EDWIN ALFRED WALFORD

EDGEHIL FROM THE KEYHOLE

The first clash of the English civil war

WITNESS TO HISTORY 006

AUTHOR:

Edwin A. Walford British Historian writer and antiquarian of Banbury, Oxfordshire.

PUBLISHING NOTE

WITNESS TO HISTORY

Our book series of history, based on eyewitnesses, or the great storytellers and war correspondents of the great events of world history: battles, sieges, military campaigns, but also travels and discoveries. New books from old books and completely revised and illustrated by Soldiershop!

1st edition: February 2017 ISBN: 9788893272070 Ebook edition ISBN 9788896519882

Title: - **Edgehill from the keyhole - The first clash of the English civil war (WTH-006)**
Based on the books: *EDGE HILL: The Battle and Battlefield. By Edwin Alfred Walford, London 1904 and OLVER CROMWELL by Samuel Rawson Gardiner, m.a. 1909*, both revised and enriched by Luca Stefano Cristini (note & color plates). Editor: Soldiershop publishing - Cover & Art Design: Luca S. Cristini. Color plates of appendix by Mario Nadir Durand.

Cover: William Harvey was deputed to look after the 12-year old Prince of Wales and the 9-year old Duke of York as witness at Edgehill

PREFACE

The Battle of Edgehill (or Edge Hill) was the first important battle of the First English Civil War. It was fought near Edge Hill and Kineton in southern Warwickshire on Sunday, 23 October 1642. All attempts at constitutional compromise between King Charles and Parliament broke down early in 1642. Both King and Parliament raised large armies to gain their way by force of arms. In October, at his temporary base near Shrewsbury, King Charles decided to march on London in order to force a decisive confrontation with Parliament's main army, commanded by the Earl of Essex. Late on 22 October, both armies unexpectedly found the enemy to be close by. The next day, the Royalist army descended from Edge Hill to force battle. After the Parliamentary artillery opened a cannonade, the Royalists attacked. Both armies consisted mostly of inexperienced and sometimes ill-equipped troops. Many men from both sides fled or fell out to loot enemy baggage, and neither army was able to gain a decisive advantage.

After the battle, King Charles resumed his march on London, but was not strong enough to overcome the defending militia before Essex's army could reinforce them.

The inconclusive result of the Battle of Edgehill prevented either faction gaining a quick victory in the war, which eventually lasted four years.

Luca Stefano Cristini

▲ The King Charles I at Edgehill

CONTENTS:

BATTLE OF EDGE HILL OCT. 23rd 1642.
72
Wellesbourne Hastings
ESSEX'S MARCH
Dene R.
Kineton
RUPERT
LINDSEY
Radway
WILMOT
Edge Hill
CHARLES'S MARCH
Warmington
Wormleighton
CHARLES'S MARCH
Edgcott
Cropredy
R. Cherwell
To Banbury
Oxhill
KINGS ARMY
PARLIAMENTARY ARMY
Scale of Miles
1 0 1 2 3
Longmans, Green & Co., London & New York.
F.S.Weller, F.R.G.S.

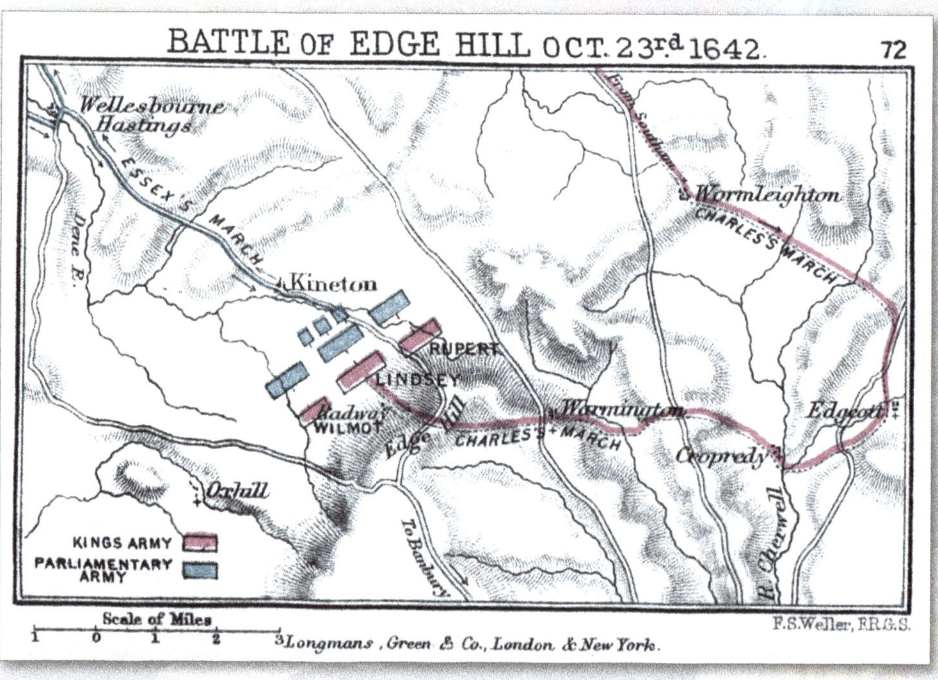

ORIGINAL PREFACE

"I go from a corruptible to an incorruptible Crown,
where no disturbance can be,
no disturbance in the world. "

Last words, said by Charles I on the scaffold before his execution. (30 January, 1649).

In In the following pages an endeavour has been made to give a concise account of the physical features of the Edge Hill district, as well as to describe the events of the first great battle of the Civil War, with which it is so intimately associated.

The intention is to provide a handbook for the guidance of the visitor rather than to attempt any elaborate historical or scientific work. Though Nugent's *"Memorials of John Hampden"* has supplied the basis of the information, Clarendon's *"History of the Great Rebellion,"* the various pamphlets of the time, and Beesley's *"History of Banbury,"* have also been freely used. In order to avoid burdening the pages with foot notes, a catalogue of works upon the subject is printed as an appendix, and the letters and numbers throughout the text refer thereto.

The catalogue, it is hoped, may be of use to the future student. The plans of the battle, based upon Nugent's account, must be looked upon as merely diagrammatic, the scale being unavoidably distorted for the purpose of showing the conjectured positions of the troops.

In the plans it may be worth note that the troops then known as *"dragooners"* are classed with the infantry. The *"Notes on Banbury and Thereabouts"* are in part reproduced from a small pamphlet published in 1879. Much of the detail relating to the older buildings has been derived from Skelton's *"Antiquities of Oxfordshire"* and Parker's descriptions in Beesley's History.

To Mr. W. L. Whitehorn my thanks are due for aid in the revision of "Edge Hill," and in the compilation of the "Notes."

Edwin A. Walford.
Banbury, July 7th, 1886.

▲ Royalist standard bearer with the color of Charles I Stuart 1642.

CHAPTER
I

▲ Prime version of van Dyck's first equestrian painting of Charles I with M. de StAntoine.

EDGE HILL: THE BATTLE AND BATTLEFIELD

To Edge Hill from Banbury a good road trends gradually up hill nearly the whole way. It rises from the 300 foot level of the Cherwell Vale to 720 at the highest ground of the ridge of the hill. At a distance of eight miles to the North-West is the edge or escarpment of high ground bounded on the East side by the vale of a tributary of the Cherwell, and on the North and West by the plain drained by the tributaries of the Avon. From Warmington, six miles from Banbury, North-Westwards to the point marked on the Ordnance Map as Knowle End, and thence South-Westwards to the Sun Rising, once the site of a hostelry on the Banbury and Stratford-on-Avon coach road, the edge makes a right angle with the apex at Knowle End.

The nearest point of the hill range is at Warmington, where a fine fourteenth century Church stands high above the rock of the roadway. There is the first record of the battle—a simple headstone to the right of the path to the South porch telling how one Captain Alexander Gourdin had died on October 24th, 1642, the day after the fight. From the church-yard long flights of steps lead to the roadway and village below, where the house tops show through the foliage of the apple orchards in which they are partly hidden. Across the vale, three miles to the North, is the range of the Burton Dassett Hills, an outlier of the Edge Hill range. The Windmill Hill, the most distant, bears the Beacon House; the square tower of Burton Dassett Church may be seen amongst the elms on the lower slopes of Church Hill; Bitham Hill appears in the foreground of the range with the pretty spire and village of Avon Dassett close at hand.

Westward of Warmington Church runs Camp Lane. It winds along the ridge, and commands wide views of the plain lands. A beautiful field path springs from the South side of the lane leading through the village of Ratley to the Round House and Ratley Grange. Facing Southwards, one looks upon an equally pleasant though more circumscribed view—the vale of Hornton.

The Arlescot Woods clothe the Northern slopes, and the Manor House rests amongst the fine trees below. The terraced fields of Adsum Hollow are three miles down vale Southward, and Nadbury Camp, supposedly a Romano-british remain, is but a remnant of similar natural terracing on the South side of the Camp Lane above Arlescot.

At Knowle End, where the road to Kineton plunges steeply down hill, is the first point of the battle ground and the commencement, strictly speaking, of Edge Hill.

A short distance down the Kineton Road, a pathway on the right leads under overspreading beech and oak trees for some distance along the crest of the Knoll, whence a good side view of the hill may be got. The gate on the opposite side of the Kineton Road opens to a path through the Radway Woods, and from it, where the foliage is less dense a prospect opens of many wide leagues of fair midland country—a veritable patchwork of field and hedgerow.

The furze below covers in part Bullet Hill, the last stand of the Royalists on the battle ground.

The road from Kineton as well as the footway through the woods leads to Edge Hill Tower, or Round House. Covering the steep hill sides are beech, elm, chestnut and lime trees of exceptionally fine growth and a wealth of common wild flowers.

The Tower or Round House is an inn, which, with a modern-antique ruin, makes as it were a landscape gardening adjunct to Radway Grange lying in the park below. From its upper room is obtained a fine view of the country. It is an octagonal tower, and was erected with artificial ruins in 1750 to mark the spot where the King's Standard was displayed before the Royalist army descended into the plain to give battle.

The village of Radway rests amongst the elms near the foot of the hill, the church spire being one of the prominent objects of the foreground. Kineton lies about four miles directly to the North, beyond which Warwick Castle may be sometimes descried, or the yet more distant spires of Coventry. Some distance from the Burton hills the smoke of the Harbury lime works drifts across the landscape. The farms Battledon and Thistledon, about midway between Radway and Kineton, marked by the coppices which almost hide the homesteads, are noted from the fact of so much of the fight having revolved round them.

The footway to the Sun Rising, 1½ miles S.W. of the Round House, follows the hill side, and though still pleasantly wooded, soon gets clear of that heavy growth of foliage which has hitherto shut out so much of the view. The eye ranges over the flat Warwickshire plain in front, to the hills of Gloucestershire and Worcestershire on the West and the North-West.

The North-Eastern outliers of the Cotteswolds, the hills of Ebrington and Ilmington, are the nearest in prominence Westwards, beyond which a clear day will allow even the distant slopes of the Malverns to be seen. The Bromsgrove, Clent and Clee hills fringe the North-West horizon, and sometimes the Wrekin is said to appear "like a thin cloud" far away.

At the point where the pathway enters the Stratford-on-Avon road stands Edge Hill House (the Sun Rising) wherein years ago were some curious relics of the fight: breast-plates, swords, matchlocks, and a sword supposed on the evidence of emblems in its decoration to have belonged to the Earl Lindsay, who commanded the royalists forces prior to the battle, and who received his death wound in the fight. In a fir coppice about 200 or 300 yards to the South of the house, the figure of a red horse roughly cut in the turf of the hill side might formerly be seen.

Dugdale gives the following account of it: "Within the Precinct of that Manour in Tysoe, now belonging to the E. of Northampton (but antiently to the Family of Stafford, as I have shewed) there is cut upon the side of Edg-Hill the Proportion of a Horse, in a very large Forme; which by Reason of the ruddy Colour of the Earth, is called The Red Horse, and gives Denomination to that fruitfull and pleasant Countrey thereabouts, commonly called The Vale of Red Horse. The

▲ A pause before the battle during the English civil war (from Marston Moor)

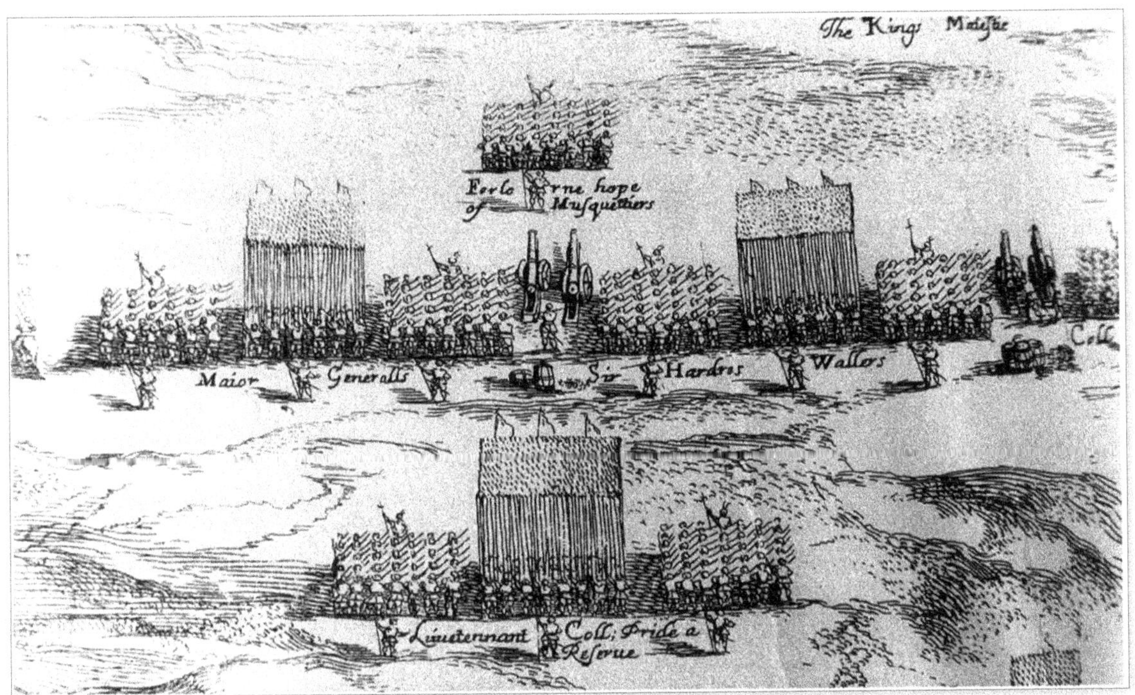

▲ Typical army formation during the XVII th century warfare

Trenches of which Ground, where the Shape of the said Horse is so cut out, being yearly scoured by a Freeholder in this Lordship, who holds certain Lands there by that service."

There is a tradition quoted by Beesley of its having been cut to commemorate the slaughter of a chieftain's horse at the battle of Towton, in 1461, the chieftain preferring to share the perils of the fight with his followers.

The reign of King Charles I. showed a widening of the difference between the ecclesiastic and puritan elements of the English community—elements which were the centres of the subsequently enlarged sections, royalist and parliamentarian. In the later dissentions between the King and the Commons it was early apparent how widespread had been the alienation of the people from the King's cause—an alienation heightened, as Green in his "Short History" tells us, by a fear that the spirit of Roman Catholicism, so victorious on the continent, should once more become dominant in England. How great was the tension may be known from the fact of the contemplated emigration to the American colonies of such leaders as Lord Saye and Sele, Lord Warwick, Lord Brooke, and Sir John Hampden and Oliver Cromwell.

When the rupture at last came, the Parliament was found to have secured the larger arsenals, and also to have forces at its disposal in the trained bands of London and in the militia, which it was enabled rapidly to enrol. Though the unfurling of the Royal Standard near Nottingham failed to secure many adherents to the King's cause, Essex hesitated to attack the royalists when they might have been easily dispersed, thinking no doubt to overawe the King by mere show of force.

Yet when Charles began recruiting in the neighbourhood of Shrewsbury, he was soon able to gather an army, and on October 12th, 1642, he commenced his march upon London.

The astute and carefully moderate policy of the Commons was to rescue the King from his surroundings, and to destroy the enemies, especially the foreign enemies, of the State, about the King's person. The sanctity of the King's person was yet a prominent factor—the belief in divinity of Kingship, notwithstanding all the misrule there had been, was yet alive in the hearts of the

▲ Portrait of Charles I Stuart (Dunfermline, 1600-London, 1649), 1626

people. Therefore when the King had gathered his forces together and began his Southward march, Lord Essex with his army was commissioned "to march against his Majesties Army and fight with them, and to rescue the persons of the King, Prince and Duke of York."
The Earl of Essex, with the Parliamentarian forces, was at that time in Worcestershire, endeavouring to prevent the recruiting of the King's troops; and though the Earl moved two days later on by rapid marches into Warwickshire, it was only to find that he had been out-marched by the King, who, after resting at Southam, stood with the Royalist army at Edgcot across the way to the capital.
That this had been accomplished, notwithstanding the opposition of the strongholds of Warwick and Coventry, speaks not unfavourably for the generalship of Earl Lindsay, the King's Lieutenant-General, whom we find at Edgcot contemplating an attack upon Banbury Castle.
The King's was a good position: it commanded all the roads to London, held Banbury in its hand, covered the Cherwell bridge and fords, and had within touch the dominating escarpment of Edge Hill. If the purpose was the subjection of some prominent leaders of the Parliamentarians it succeeded only in the taking of Lord Saye and Sele's house at Broughton, and of Banbury, and Banbury Castle; in the partial destruction of Lord Spencer's house at Wormleighton, and in sending a summons to Warwick Castleto surrender.
Kineton, on October 22nd, was the headquarters of the Parliamentary army, the troops in the evening disposing themselves on the surrounding plain.
"The common soldiers have not come into a bed, but lain in the open field in the wet and cold nights," says the Worthy Divine "and most of them scarcely eat or drank at all for 24 hours together, nay, for 48, except fresh water when they could get it."
The want of transport, which had necessitated Hampden and Hollis struggling behind a day's march in the rear in the neighbourhood of Stratford-on-Avon, had no doubt entailed these privations upon the army. Nor do the Royalists appear to have fared better, for Clarendon complains of the hostility of the country people, stating also that the circuit in which the battle was fought, being between the dominions of Lord Saye and Lord Brooke, was the most eminently corrupt of any in the kingdom.
The King's forces seem to have been quartered about the country between Wormleighton and Cropredy, Prince Rupert with his cavalry near Wormleighton, the King himself staying at Edgcot House, whilst the main body of the army occupied the slopes and high lands on the Northamptonshire side of the Cherwell vale near by.
Thus the three roads North of Banbury were dominated by the Royalist troops, and the fourth, the old London road, was within striking distance.
The preaching of the local divines, Robert Harris, John Dod, and Robert Cleaver, had no doubt added largely to the enthusiasm of the country folk for the cause of the Commons.
Though no great increase of the King's forces could be expected in such a district, yet there is an interesting account in Kimber and Johnson's Baronetage (1771) of a country gentleman Mr. (afterwards Sir Richard) Shuckburgh: "Sir Richard Shuckburgh, Knt., eldest son and heir, was in no way inferior to his ancestors.
As King Charles I. marched to Edgecot, near Banbury, on October 22nd, 1642, he saw him hunting in the fields with a very good pack of hounds, upon which it is reported that he fetched a deep sigh, and asked who the gentleman was that hunted so merrily that morning when he was going to fight for his crown and dignity; and being told that it was this Richard Shuckburgh, he was graciously ordered to be called to him, and was by him very graciously received.
Upon which he went immediately home, armed all his tenants, and the next day attended him in the field, where he was knighted, and was present at the battle of Edge Hill.
After the taking of Banbury Castle, and his Majesty's retreat from those parts, he went to his own seat and fortified himself on the top of Shuckborough Hill, where, being attacked by some of the

Parliament forces, he defended himself till he fell, with most of his tenants about him; but being taken up and life perceived in him, he was carried away prisoner to Kenilworth Castle, where he lay a considerable time, and was forced to purchase his liberty at a dear rate."

A fight for the possession of Lord Spencer's house at Wormleighton was the Saturday evening's prelude to the Sunday's battle. It had been garrisoned by some Parliamentarian troops sent by Essex, and in Rupert's attack some prisoners were taken, from whom, it is said, the whereabouts of the Parliamentarian army was learned.

The house is said to have been partly burned down in the fight, but it is not clear whether it happened then or in the year 1643. Though with the Parliamentarians in the early part of the Rebellion, Lord Spencer became Royalist long ere the campaigns were over.

The fact of an outpost being pushed so far as Wormleighton shows that the Dassett Hills were held by the Parliament forces. The Royalists had marched into the heart of a hostile country, Warwick Castle and Lord Brooke on the N.W., Fawsley House and the Knightleys on the N.E., and on the South, Sir A. Cope and Hanwell Castle, and Banbury and Broughton Castle.

Lord Northampton's lands on the Western border of Oxfordshire were near enough to find touch with the King. His house played locally a most prominent part for the Royalist cause, and its military leadership was of the best

Early on the morning of Sunday, October 23rd, Prince Rupert forwarded information to the King that the camp fires of the Parliamentarian army had been seen on the plain between Edge Hill and Kineton. With keen foresight Earl Lindsay abandoned the intended advance upon Banbury, and speedily began the movement of the Royalist army towards the fringe of hills which dominates the Warwickshire vale. It seems at first strange that the Parliamentarians, familiar as so many of them were with the physical features of the neighbourhood, should have neglected when so near to secure possession of some part of the Edge Hill ridge.

This, however, is explained in a pamphlet of the time, "An Exact and True Relation of the Dangerous and Bloudy Fight between his Majestie's Army and the Parliament near KeyntoTherein we learn that the artillery were unready, for want of draught horses, and with Colonel Hampden and Colonel Grantham were forced to be left behind, and hence no advance could safely be made beyond Keynton.

Hampden had with him three regiments of foot, nine or ten troops of horse, some companies of dragooners, and seven pieces of cannon, with the necessary ammunition train, perhaps about 4,000 men in all. The troops of the Parliament were quartered in the villages of the plain.

Tradition says that Tysoe was occupied, and that the soldiers took the bread from the village ovens ere they marched down street to the fight. But of the doings at Compton in the Hole, barely a mile distant, during the occupation we know nothing. It is hard also to understand that there should have been anything in the nature of a surprise in the Royalist advance, for within a district so sympathetic to their cause, one would have supposed the Puritan leaders to have been immediately informed of every movement of their enemies.

Indeed, in another quaint pamphlet, "A Letter sent from a Worthy Divine," the writer says that the alarm came at about eight o'clock in the morning, that the enemy were advancing, and that "it pleased God to make myself the first instrument of giving a certain discovery of it, by the help of a perspective glass, from the top a hill."

Deploying, therefore, before daybreak, across Cropredy Bridge, then narrower than at present, and no doubt crossing the Cherwell at certain fords also, the King's forces marched by way of Mollington to Warmington, where they had been preceded by Prince Rupert's horse, who would have travelled across the Southern part of the Dassett Hills. It is said that "the foot were quartered at so great distance that many regiments marched seven or eight miles to the rendezvous, so that

▲ King Charles I addresses his officers in September 1642: Battle of Edgehill 23rd October 1642

it was past one of the clock before the King's forces marched down hill." Much delay would be occasioned in getting the troops across the river Cherwell, not so easy to be forded at that time of the year.

The narrow bridge would allow but slow passage for 10,000 or 12,000 men, with all the impedimenta of war material. Another pamphleteer says "the King's horse were at the rendezvous between ten and eleven; the van of the foot an hour later, and the rear and artillery, including the Lord Lt. General's own regiment, not until two hours after."

As the Parliamentarian troops take up their position upon the plain, it is worth while to pause for a few minutes to look at the composition and armament of the two forces.

Many of the troops on both sides appear to have been indifferently provided with weapons. Implements of warfare that had not been in use since the Wars of the Roses—the long bow, the cross bow, &c.—resumed their places amongst the accoutrements of the men at arms.

There were the heavy horse in iron casques, breast-plates and greaves, the musketeers with their matchlocks, and the dragoons or dragooners, with sword and matchlock.

These last seem to have been so called from the drake, the firearm they once carried, and though not strictly speaking cavalry, yet accompanying and supporting them. Each regiment of Lord Essex's army carried a standard inscribed on the one side with the watchword of the Parliament, "God with us," and on the other side the motto of the regimental commander; Lord Saye and Sele's were the blue coats, the Commander's were orange and Lord Broke's purple; Colonel Ballard's troops were clad in grey, Colonel Holles' in red, and Lord Mandeville's in blue.

Across his breastplate each officer of the Parliamentary army wore an orange scarf, the commander's colour.

There were on the side of the Parliament eleven regiments of foot, forty-two troops of horse, and 700 dragoons, numbering according to Nugent about 13,000, though the officers in their account place their strength as low as 10,000, which may have meant prior to the arrival of Hampden with the artillery and rear troops.

The Royalist army is stated to have possessed 1,000 horse and 4,000 foot more; in all 14,000 foot and 4,000 horse and dragoons—but as very few troops were of full compliment the numbers were no doubt over estimated. The full strength of a foot regiment was 1,200, of a troop of horse about 120 and of dragooners about the same number to each company.

The Red and the Blue Regiments of the King's foot were so named from the colour of their uniforms, the former being the King's foot guards. In cavalry, however, it was that the Royalist army was predominant—more so, perhaps, from the quality of the material than from any superiority of equipment, Prince Rupert's show troop being a prominent example.

Cromwell, in a speech before Parliament, bore testimony on this point, explaining his reconstruction of the army as having arisen from the fact that "such base and mean fellowes," tapsters and serving men as they then had, not being "able to encounter gentlemen that had honour and courage and resolution in them, He strove to find such as had the spirit of God in them." Towards mid-day the royalist army had occupied the whole length of the brow of the hill between the Sun Rising and Arlescot; the left wing at the Sun Rising, the centre at about the point where the Round House now stands and the right wing at Knowle End, where the road to Kineton descends the hill. Well had it been for the King had the advice of so able a soldier as Earl Lindsay prevailed at the council of war over the more impetuous policy of Rupert.

He had the strong position of the hill crest, with convenient roads for the rapid movement of troops, and, moreover, natural advantages which would have masked those movements.

Essex would have hesitated to risk the assault of a position of such strength, especially when defended by a force greater than his own. These advantages were, however, abandoned for the more dashing policy of Rupert to descend to the plain and at once give battle. It must not be forgotten, however, that the knowledge of the enemy's artillery with part of the army being far in the rear, but approaching with what speed they could, and the difficulty of provisioning the army in a hostile district, would give weight to Rupert's counsel. Brilliant cavalry officer as he undoubtedly was, his defiance of control caused the Earl to resign his command, and the disposition of the forces to devolve upon Earl Ruthven, and so he decided against the King the fortunes of the then commencing war. The Parliamentarians had in the meantime not been idle.

Turning aside from church, whither they had been going, the divines encouraged the soldiers as they stood drawn up ready for the fight. Poor retrenchment as they were said to have had, the ground lent itself to preparation for defence: the thick growth of furze tied and wattled together on the gently sloping upland: (the old phrase a "good bush whacking" may point to its service in fight). Also there was the long ditch with its wet clay banks covering the front.

It is certain that a large number of the force were fighting on their own ground and for their own homes. Evidence shows how heavy the fight was thereabouts.

The centre consisted of three regiments of infantry, including one of the general's, under Lord Brooke and Colonel Ballard, another regiment, under Colonel Holles, being in the rear.

These faced the Battledon Farm, about one mile North-West of Radway, and on some rising ground to the right the artillery was posted. The right wing moved towards the Sun Rising.

It was composed of four brigades of horse, under Sir John Meldrum, Col. Stapleton, and Sir William Balfore (the divisional general), with Col. Fielding's brigade and some guns in the rear. Capt.

▲ Portrait of palatins Princes Charles Louis Ist électeur (1617-1680) and his brother Rupert (1619-1682) Louvre by A. van dick 1637

Fiennes' regiment was with this wing, which was covered on the right by some musketeers. Captain Oliver Cromwell fought there also. Infantry, including the Oxfordshire Militia under Sir William Constable and Lord Roberts, took up the intervening space between the centre and the right wing.
The cavalry of the left wing, covering the Kineton road, was made up of twenty-four troops, under Sir James Ramsay: the infantry in five regiments, officered by Cols. Essex and Chomley and Lords Wharton and Mandeville, with Sir Wm. Fairfax in reserve, occupied the ground between the cavalry and the main body. A few guns were placed in the rear of the horse.
Imposing indeed must the sight have been in bright sunlight of that early Sunday afternoon as the Royalist troops, began to descend the hill side!
The slopes do not appear to have been so thickly wooded as they are now, and the unenclosed country, without the many obstacles of fence and hedgerow, offered all that a cavalry officer could desire for the exercise of his art and arm.
Before this the King had summoned the officers to the royal tent, and in his brief speech had said: "My Lords and Gentlemen here present,—If this day shine prosperously for us, we shall be happy in a glorious victory. Your King is both your cause, your quarrel, and your captain.
The foe is in sight. Now show yourselves no malignant parties, but with your swords declare what

▲ The Edgehill battlefield today.

courage and fidelity is within you. Come life or death, your King will bear you company, and ever keep this field, this place, and this day's service in his grateful remembrance."

The King, wearing a black velvet mantle over his armour, and steel cap covered with velvet on his head, rode along the lines of his troops and spoke to them: "Matters are now to be declared with swords, not by words." Perhaps, however, the most beautiful of these records is that of the truly soldier-like prayer of Lord Lindsay, "O Lord, Thou knowest how busy I must be this day; if I forget Thee do not Thou forget me."

CHAPTER II

▲ A royal cornet at horse

BATTLE OF EDGE HILL
(COMMENCEMENT OF BATTLE)

The The King's centre, under General Ruthven, moved forward as far as the village of Radway. The six columns of infantry of which it was composed were under the divisional command of Sir Edmund Verney and Sir Jacob Astley; Earl Lindsay and Lord Willoughby led their Lincolnshire regiment. Between these and the right wing were eight other regiments of infantry. The cavalry of the right wing, under Prince Rupert, commenced slowly the steep descent of the road through Arlescot wood and the Kineton road, the base of which is known as the Bullet Hill, and drew up there in a meadow at the bottom of the hill.

Fiennes states that the better opportunity for the Parliamentarian attack would have been before the artillery and rear came down the hill, which they were a long time in doing.

The left wing rested upon the Sun Rising, Col. Ennis and Col. Lisle's dragoons covering the flank; near by were the Welsh soldiers and Carnarvon's regiments of pikemen.

In advance Wilmot's two regiments of horse were working across the Vale of the Red Horse, Digby's reserve covering the crest of the hill.

Lord Essex's artillery were the first to break the peace of the day, a challenge immediately replied to by the Royalist guns near Radway. Wilmot, of Adderbury, made the first aggressive movement in a charge upon the Parliamentarian right, and though some success seems to have attended it, yet it can scarcely have been of so much importance as Clarendon the Royalist historian makes out, for he writes: "The left wing, commanded by Wilmot, had a great success, though they had to charge in worse ground, amongst hedges and through gaps and ditches which were lined with musketeers. Sir A. Aston, with great courage and dexterity, beat off these musketeers with his dragoons; and then the right wing of their horse 'was easily dispersed, and fled the chase fearlessly.'

The reserve, seeing none of the enemy's horse left, thought there was nothing more to be done but to pursue those that fled, and could not be contained by their commanders, but with spurs and loose reins followed the chase which the left wing had led them.

Thus while victory was unquestionable, the King was left in danger from the reserve of the Parliament, which, pretending to be friends, broke in upon the foot, and did great execution."

Certainly in charge and counter charge at this stage of the attack, the Parliamentarians show to no advantage, and the dispersal of the dragoons, musketeers, and part of Fielding's horse, seems to have taken place, but the subsequent successful charge of Balfour's and Stapleton's brigades makes it clear that they were not involved in any disaster.

On the right wing, soon after the time of Wilmot's charge near the Sun Rising, Rupert's troops moved down the foot of the hill in the direction of the Kineton road and towards Ramsay's horse, which advanced to meet them.

The Parliamentary general had lined the hedgerows on his flank with musketeers, and had placed ranks of musketeers between his horse. But as the cavaliers swept down the slope a defect was visible in the Parliamentarian ranks, and Sir Faithful Fortescue's Irish troop threw off their orange scarves and deserted bodily, not quite soon enough, it seems, to save themselves, for a score or so of saddles were emptied in the onrush of Rupert's cavaliers.

The roundhead ranks were disordered, for the troops had fired their long pieces wildly, and scarcely waiting the meeting, they fled, leaving the musketeers to be cut up.

The troops of cavaliers swept through them scattering and destroying all in their way; then deflecting a little to the left they pressed back the mass of fugitives upon the foot regiments of Essex, Mandeville and Chomley which in turn were overthrown, and the artillery captured. Even Wharton's regiment and Fairfax's reserve were hurled back. Ramsay, the cavalry general, was carried for two miles in the melee, and with some of his troopers found a way through the hostile lines to Banbury.Rupert continued in unsparing pursuit even into the streets of Kineton and as far as Chadshunt.

Thus was the left wing of Lord Essex's army dispersed, though to reform for a later phase of the fight. After so much success the baggage proved to be too attractive to the victors, and had the time wasted in plundering been spent in an attack upon the rear of the Parliamentarian army, then the reign of Charles Stuart might have had a less tragic ending.

But with all this, it must be borne in mind that the incident of the rolling up of a wing was repeated in other battles of the war which were more disastrous to the King's cause. Sir James Ramsay at a Court Martial at St. Albans in November of the same year made a vindication of his conduct.

An amusing letter from Captain Kightley tells of this phase of the fight. He admits that in part his own regiment ran away, and it seems to be probable that Captain John Fiennes was in no better way, though in the subsequent rally and attack upon Prince Rupert both did very good service.

The right wing of the Puritan forces had in the meantime become aggressive. It was the beginning of the great turning movement which was repeated in each of the great battles of the war by the Parliamentarians, in fact, so evident at Naseby and Marston Moor, as to compel belief in studied uniformity of plan.

▲ The starting of a battle in the mid XVII th century

The abandonment or weakening of one wing, then the use of all the weight of the other wing with the foot as a centre pivot, to out-flank, attack, and crush in succession the opposing wing and centre of the Royalist army. Balfore, Meldrum, and Stapleton's brigades charged Wilmot's cavalry with such vigour that these were thrust back upon the three regiments of pikemen, under Lord Carnarvon, and chased up the hill side.

Cannon balls and other remains of the fight found on the hill slopes at Lower Westcote near the Sun Rising are evidence of this attack. The infantry under Roberts and Constable having moved forward to aid in the attack upon Carnarvon, now wheeled upon the King's centre, which soon became the focus of a fierce and bloody fight, for the elated Roundhead horse, after crushing in the Royalist left wing, hurled themselves also upon the flanks of the nearest troops of the King's centre, and the blue-coated Broughton horsemen had a busy time of it amongst the royalist gunners as they rode through the battery. Earl Lindsay's Lincolnshire regiment, which he had led pike in hand, received the brunt of the attack; it was overpowered, and the unfortunate general left for dead with a musket ball in his thigh.

The Red Regiment moved up in support, only in turn to be cut up and almost annihilated, and Lord Willoughby was made prisoner also in the attempt to rescue his father the Earl.

Then followed a brilliant personal fight for the royal standard, but the Puritan horseman Copley cut down Sir Edmund Verney, knight marshal of the King's horse, and standard bearer, and secured the prize. The success of this attack was largely brought about by the ruse alluded to, where, "pretending to be friends," they broke in upon the King's regiments.

If it is true that they got so near as to shake hands, the business must have been very simple.

Verney had presentiment of his death, and the severed hand clasping the standard shaft is said to be yet sadly searched for by the ghost of Claydon House.

On the finger of the hand was a ring, a king's gift. Nugent says about the standard's recapture: "The Royal standard was taken by Mr. Young, one of Sir William Constable's ensigns, and delivered by Lord Essex to his own Secretary, Chambers, who rode by his side. Elated by the prize, the Secretary rode about, more proudly than wisely, waving it round his head.

Whereupon in the confusion, one of the King's officers, Captain Smith, of the Lord John Stewart's troop, seeing the standard captured, threw round him the orange scarf of a fallen Parliamentarian, and riding in among the lines of his enemies, told the Secretary that 'it were a shame that so honourable a trophy of war should be borne by a penman.'

To which suggestions the credulous guardian of this honourable trophy consenting, surrendered it to the disguised cavalier, who galloped back with it amain, and before evening received knighthood under its shadow."

Brooke's, Hollis', and Ballard's infantry, moved across part of the ground abandoned by Ramsay's horse to attack the right flank of the King's centre, an attack which soon becomes as disastrous to the Royalists as that on the other flank where Lindsay has fallen.

In fact, the regiments of foot from the Parliamentary rear with Constable's infantry and Stapleton's horse, made a combined assault upon the King's centre, which they commenced breaking up.

In vain were the royalist reserves hurried forward. The Blue Regiment was cut off by Sir Arthur Haselrigge. Stapleton made a dash, and the King, who had been watching the fickle fortunes of his soldiers from a mound (now the King's Clump) near Radway, narrowly escaped being made a prisoner.

The timely interference of a body of royalist horse—an interference not of sufficient weight to stop the tide of the Puritan attack, but only to stay it for a few moments—enabled the King to gain the shelter of the hill, whither also the fragments of some of his regiments are compelled to follow.

▲ The Eve of the Battle of Edge Hill, 1642 a paint of Charles Landseer .

BATTLE OF EDGE HILL

Advance of Hampden and Retreat of Rupert & King

Meanwhile Rupert had been lost to sight in Kineton streets. When he learned that the fortunes of the day were, in other parts of the field, in full flow against his cause, he and his cavaliers re-formed for the retreat. The place is still known as Prince Rupert's Headland.

There was, however, another factor to be taken into consideration. Some of Hampden's green-coated soldiers, stimulated no doubt by the sounds of the fight, had in the meantime come up from Stratford-on-Avon, and were prepared to dispute Rupert's return.

They also succeeded in re-forming many of the fugitives, in which duty Captains Cromwell, Nathaniel Fiennes and Kightley, took part. The guns and infantry opened fire upon the retreating cavaliers, who had a hard fight to regain the hill butt, for Stapleton's horse, after fighting along the whole of the Royalist line, chased them home. Nevertheless, two of the royal regiments refused to be beaten; falling back upon their guns, they made a stand, probably along the line from Radway to Bullet Hill, and there, reinforced by Rupert's returning troops, they held their ground, repulsing the Parliamentarian attacks, and so says Fiennes, "horse and foot stood together against horse and foot until night, when the Royalists retired up hill."

It is probably from this stage of the fight that Bullet Hill got its name. The braided lovelock of many a cavalier who rode so exultingly down the hill in the afternoon sunlight had a stain of a far deeper colour 'ere sunset, and with the phase of the fight following the straggling return of Rupert's Horse, the events of the day seem to have ended.

The King would have tried a final charge with some unbroken regiments to test once more the fortunes of the day, but was with difficulty persuaded from so perilous an enterprise. Each side claims that only the night prevented a completely victorious issue for its cause, but when we consider that the right wing and centre of the King's army were disorganised, and in part driven up the hill, and that the Parliamentarians were in possession of the battle ground, the Royalists retaining possession only of the low ground from Radway to Bullet Hill, it seems that the advantage rested on the Puritan side. One remained master of the field of battle, the other kept the London road.

Amongst the several estimates of the slain, it is hard to say which is nearest the truth. Clarendon gives the number as 5,000, two parts of whom were Parliamentarian, and one part the King's, but the probability is that it was nearer, a half of that number.

Fiennes puts down the losses acknowledged by the Royalists themselves as 2,000.

Certainly the records show that they were exceptionally heavy in officers, one writer adducing as a reason that "the rebel officers had fleeter horses, so not so many of them were slain." During the cold frosty night after the battle the wounded must of necessity have been left exposed, inasmuch as the fight stretched over many miles of country, and was continued until night; nor do the Royalists appear to have been debarred from searching for their wounded, as we learn by the succour of old Sir Gervase Scroop by his son.

The King's troops says Clarenden "had not the shelter of tree or hedge, and after a very cold night spent on the field, without any refreshment of victual or provision for the soldiers (for the country was so disaffected that it not only sent no provisions, but many soldiers who straggled into the villages for relief were knocked on the head by the common people), the King found his troops very thin." The Parliamentarians, whose baggage had been cut up by Rupert, could not have been in much better plight; some of them, however, fired the Dassett Beacon, and the news of the conflict was thus flashed across country to London.

Though so much is recorded of Mr. Wilmot's (afterwards Lord Rochester, of Adderbury,) position and work during the day, nothing other than the mere statement is made of a far greater leader, Spencer Compton, Earl of Northampton, than that he was at Edge Hill, with some of the best disciplined men. It would seem that the extended movement of the Royalist forces along the hill ridge in the early part of the day was to give support to Compton Wynyate, or get aid therefrom.

It was but three miles distant. Whether any deflection of Hampden's force moving from Stratford-on-Avon was made to mask or retard Compton's men is mere surmise: the main part of Hampden's rear did not reach the field until the Sunday midnight, when Essex got reinforced by a regiment of horse and two of foot. The story of successive campaigns, as in this the first fight, resolves itself into the superiority of the heavy armament of the Parliamentarian horse.

The improved status of the men added greater force at a later date. With all the dash, and all the value of the light horse of the King for foray, when in the field the cavalier went down before the iron armed horse of the Parliament's army. On the following day, the two armies again drew up, the Parliamentarians having in the early morning retired from the hill side towards Kineton, but neither showed any disposition to renew the fight.

Essex was pressed to do so by some of his more impetuous officers, but wanted the daring necessary for so bold a movement. Charles sent a messenger into the rebel lines with a pardon for Earl Essex, which "messenger returned with so great a sense of danger as not to have observed the number and disposition of the Parliamentary forces." Later on, Essex retired to Warwick with his troops, and Prince Rupert is reported to have followed, but failed to overtake them, though it is stated that he destroyed many wagons and carriages with munitions, &c.

The reconnaissance appears to have been otherwise fruitless, for the King at once marched southward, and received the surrender of Banbury Castle, and also subsequently of Broughton Castle. Lord Saye, Sir Wm. Cobb, of Adderbury, and John Doyley, Esq., were not only proclaimed

▲ A battle during the English civil war.

traitors, but were specially exempted from the King's pardon. The position of the graves in which the slain were buried is about 200 yards south of Thistle Farm, the ground bearing still the name of the Grave Field, and a wych elm marks the site of one of the graves. The part that Oliver Cromwell played in the struggle has not unnaturally been the cause of much comment.

Carlyle characteristically cuts the Gordian knot with the statement, "Captain Cromwell was present, and did his duty, let angry Denzil say what he will." Denzil Hollis's charge that Cromwell purposely absented himself from the field may be fairly set aside on the ground of malice, his enmity being openly shown, and moreover it meets contradiction in Cromwell's own statement: "At my first going out into this engagement, I saw our men were beaten at every hand.

I did indeed." Neither can Dugdale's account of Cromwell's hurried descent from a church steeple by means of the bell rope, when he saw the Parliamentarian disaster, be received in the face of the letter written by Captain Nathaniel Fiennes, which ends thus: "These persons underwritten were all of the Right wing and never stirred from their Troops, but they and their Troops fought till the last minute. The Lord Generall's Regiment—Sir Philip Stapleton, Captain Draper, Serjeant Major Gunter, Lord Brookes, Captain Sheffield, Captain Temple, Captain Cromwell; Sir William Belfore's Regiment—Sir William Belfore, Serjeant Major Hurrey, Lord Grey, Captain Nathaniell Fiennes, Sir Arthur Hasilrigge, Captain Longe." It is equally curious that Captain Oliver Cromwell, of Troop Sixty-Seven, was at Edge Hill in the place he invariably occupied during the civil war, viz., with the victorious wing, and that the history of the fluctuations of the fight should be repeated in so many of the great battles, Naseby and Marston Moor to wit.

CHAPTER III

▲ The roundhead cavalry of parliamentary army.

CONTEMPORARY RELATION OF THE BATTLE

A most true and Exact
RELATION OF BOTH THE BATTELS FOUGHT BY HIS EXCELLENCY
and his Forces against the bloudy Cavelliers.
The one on the 23 of October last near Keynton below Edge-Hill in Warwickshire, the other at Worcester by Colonell Brown, Captain Nathaniel, and John Fiennes, and Colonell Sands and some others.
Wherein the particulars of each Battel is punctually set down at large for the full satisfaction of all people, with the Names of the Commanders and Regiments that valiently stood it out.
Also the number and Names of the Chief Commanders that were slain on both sides: All which is here faithfully set down without favour or partiality to either Army.

Written by a worthy Captain Master Nathaniel Fiennes, And commanded to be Printed.

London, Printed for Joseph Hunscott
Novem. 9. 1642.

Mr. Nathaniel Fiennes his Letter to his Father

My Lord, I have sent to your Lordship a Relation of the last Battell fought in Keynton Field, which I shewed to the Generall and Lievtenant Generall of the Horse, and divers Colonels and Officers, and they conceive it to be right and according to the truth: For the ill writing of it, I desire that your Lordship would excuse me, for I had not time to write it over again; yet I suppose it may be read, and your Lordship may cause it to be written faire, if your Lordship thinke it worth so much.

For that which your Lordship writeth concerning my brother John, is a most false and malicious slander which that fellow hath raised upon him, that he should be the first man that fled on the left wing, when as none of your Lordship's sonnes were in the left wing, and my brother John was not at all in the field while the fight was; for by occasion that I intreated him on Saturday morning, when we marched towards Keynton (little dreaming of a Battell the next day) to go to Evesham (which was but three miles from the quarter where our Troops lay, before they marched with the Army to Keynton) for to take some Arms that were come thither the night before, for such of our men as wanted Arms, and so to come after to the Rendevous at Keynton.

He could not come thither on Saturday with those men of both Troops which went backe with him to Evesham for their Arms, but the next day he came thither between three or foure of the clock; at which time our left wing being defeated, many of the Runaways met with him as he was coming to the Army; and happily among the rest, this fellow that raised this report; for that Vivers which your Lordship mentioneth, was not Captain Vivers (for he was in Banbury) but a brother of his that was in one of Colonell Goodwin's Troops, and as I heard my brother say, he saw him there; and I heard my Lord Generall say, that Vivers was one of the first that ran away: Now it seemes that those men that ran away so timely, seeing my brother before them, reported as if he had fled from the Army, which is so contrary to the truth, that he tooke a great deale of pains to make his own men and Captain Vivers' men which were with him to stand, and to stop the Runaways that came from the Army, and this he did, and made two or three stands, and at length gathered a pretty body upon

▲ The assault at the baggage.

a hill together, and with them (there being Captain Keightlye's, and Captain Cromwell's Troope, at length came to them also) he marched towards the Town; and hearing the enemy was there (as indeed they were with the greatest part of their horse they made a stand, and sending forth their Scouts to give them intelligence where the enemy and where our Forces were, at length they came to knowledge of Colonell Hampden's Brigado that was coming another way to the Town, and so joyning themselves unto them, they came to the Army together.

My Lord Generall is very sensible of the wrong that this fellow hath done my brother, and will inquire after him to have him punished, as he hath written to my Lord Wharton concerning him, to let you know so much. Master Bond whom he citeth for one of his authors, denies that ere he spake to my brother at all, or that he saw any such thing of flying, as that base fellow reporteth, and this your Lordship shall have under his hand. It had been a strange thing if my brother that shewed so much courage at Worcester, should have been so faint-hearted on this occasion; But I strange that men will give credit to every idle fellow; if they will, they may heare that my Lord Generall and all the Officers, every one of them ran away.

But my Lord, as your Lordship hath great cause to be thankfull, together with us, to God, that in all these late actions of danger, hath preserved the persons and lives of all your three Sons, so also for preserving their honors, and the honor of Religion; that in this cause they have never flinsht, but have all of them in their severall places and conditions been as forward to hazard their persons into the midst of their's and God's enemies as any whosever.

And of the truth of this (though we do not vapour so much as some do) there are enough, and those very honorable witnesses that can and will affirm it as well as

Your Lordship's most obedient Son,

NATHANIEL FIENNES

A most true Relation of the Battell fought by his Excellency and his Forces against the bloudy Cavalliers

The two and twentieth of October, being Saturday, his Excellency the Earl of Essex came with twelve regiments of Foot, and two and forty Troops of Horse, and a part of the Ammunition and Artillery, to Keynton, a little Market Toun, almost in the mid-way between Stratford upon the Avon, and Banbury, there being three Regiments of Foot, and nine or ten Troops of Horse, with seven Pieces of Cannon, and good store of Ammunition coming after, together with six Companies of Dragooners; the Dragooners, and two of the Regiments of Foot, with the Cannon, and nine or ten Troops of Horse, came to Keynton on Sunday night, a little before the day went down; The Regiment, with the Lord Rochfords, came not into the Army till Monday in the afternoon.

The King's Army was lodged on Saturday night, about Croprede and Edgecot, some 6 or 7 miles from Keynton; and having, no doubt, got intelligence that part of our Army, and Artillery, with a great part of our Ammunition was behinde us, they thought they could not have a better opportunity to fight with our Army, especially if they could get the advantage of the hill before us, it being a very high and steep assent, which if they were put to the worst might serve them for a Retreat, as it did, it being that which saved them, their Carriages, and the Colours of their Regiments of Foot that ran away; for of those that fought it out, we tooke most of them, excepting onely those two Regiments that stood it out till night, and went off with their horse in an orderly way.

The enemy having resolved to give us Battell, and no whit doubting of the Victory, they being more then we were, both in horse and foot (a considerable Brigado of our Army being behinde) and having a great opinion of the resolution of their Souldiers, wherein they were partly deceived, and partly not, as it hapned also on our side; They returned back towards Edge Hill, and made all possible speed to gain the hill before us (which they did, by reason that his Excellency had not timely intelligence of their designe, otherwise we were much neerer the hill, and might have been possessed of it before them).

And by that time our Army was drawn out of the Town about a mile and half towards the hill, the Dragooners, and some of the enemie's Foot were coming down the hill; Their horse having gotten down most of them on their right hand, and placed themselves in a fair Meadow, at the bottom of the hill; Their Cannon and Ammunition, with the Rere of their foot, were something long ere they came down.

And if we had charged them before their Cannon and all their Foot were come down, we might have had a great advantage: but they got all down into the Meadow at the foot of the hill, and there drew up their Army very handsomely, their horse being on their right Wing for the most part, and their Dragooners, and some few Troops of horse on their left Wing; some of their prisoners said they had four Regiments of horse on that wing also; but I could never speak with any of our Army, that either saw any such number of horse, or could tell what they did, unlesse they went directly to Keynton, to plunder the Carriages without charging our Army at all.

For our Army, it was drawn up upon a little rising ground, and being amongst the horse, I could not well discern how the foot were drawn up; only I knew they were most of them a good space behinde the horse, when we began to charge: but for the horse, there were three Regiments on the right Wing of our Army, viz., The Lord Generalls Regiment commanded by Sir Philip Stapleton; Sir William Belfore's Regiment, Lieutenant Generall of the Horse; and the Lord Fielding's Regiment, which stood behinde the other two, in the way of a reserve.

On the right Wing of our Army, was Sir James Ramsey, with some 24 Troops, for many of our Troops were not in the Field that day.

The Armies being thus placed one against another with no great oddes of the winde or ground (but

▲ Fight for the standard at Edgehill

what their was of winde the enemies had it, the ground being reasonable indifferent on both sides) after many shot of Cannon which did very little hurt amongst us, and very much amongst them, their foot advancing for the most part against our right Wing, and their horse against the left Wing of our Army.

Their horse had the better of our horse that were on our left Wing, and routing them, drove them back upon our foot, and amongst the rest, upon Colonell Hollis his Regiment, which was in the Rere, and they brake through it, yet they ran not away, nor seemed to be at all dismayed at it; but four other Regiments ran away, and fought not at all, and many of them cast away their Colours, and so the enemy took them up, having scarce got so much as one Colour or Cornet of those Regiments or Troops that fought, whereas all the Colours that we got from them, and the King's

Standard, which we had a long time in our possession, were taken out of the midst of their best Regiments that fought it out very resolutely: Our left Wing being thus put to the worst, the day was very desperate on our side; and had not God clearly fought for us, we had lost it; for had the enemie's horse when they routed the left Wing, fallen upon the Rere of our right Wing, in all probability the army had been wholly defeated: But they made directly to the Town, and there falling upon our Carriages, most barbarously massacred a number of poor Waggoners and Carters that had no arms to defend themselves, and so fell to pillaging and pursuing those that ran away, so long till they met with Colonell Hampden, who with the other Brigado of the Army (which came with the Artillery and Ammunition which was behinde) was by this time come near to Keynton, and the enemie's Troops falling upon him as they pursued our men that ran away, he gave them a stop, and discharging five pieces of Cannon against them, he slew some of them; whereupon they returned in some fear and disorder: But when they came back into the Field, they found all their Infantry, excepting two Regiments, cut in pieces or defeated and run away; for it pleased God to put such courage into four or five of our Regiments of foot, and two Regiments of horse, the Lord Generall's commanded by Sir Philip Stapleton, and Sir William Belfore, that they defeated all their Regiments of foot, except two.

Sir William Belfore's Regiment of horse charged a Regiment of the enemie's foot, before any foot came up to assist him, and breaking into it cut most of it off; and after, by the assistance of some of our foot, he defeated another Regiment, and so we got up to the greatest part of the enemies Ordnance, and took them, cutting off the Geers of the horses that drew them, and killing the Gunners under the Carriages, but were forced to leave them without any to guard them, by reason we were fain to make good the day against severall Regiments of foot that still fought with a good deal of resolution; especially that which was of the King's Guard, where his Standard was, close by which Sir William Belfore's Regiment rode when they came from taking the Ordnance; and they taking us to be their friends, and we them, some of our Company, shook hands with some of them, which was the cause that after riding up towards the Lord Generall's Regiment of horse, they gave fire upon Sir William Belfore's Regiment, and discerning each other to be friends, we joyned Companies; and so with half the Lord Generall's Regiment, which his Excellency himself led up, charging the King's Regiment, we defeated it, took the Standard, took the Generall of the King's Army, the Earl of Lindley, and his son, and Colonell Vavasor who was Lieutenant Colonell of that Regiment, and killed Sir Edward Varney upon the place (who carryed the Standard), Colonell John Munroe, and divers others: In this charge, and generally throughout the day, the Lord Generall's Troop, consisting most of Gentlemen, carried themselves most valiantly; and had all our Troops, of our left Wing been made of the same metall, the enemy had not made so easie an impression into them. And what is said of my Lord Generall's Troop, may most truly, and to his high praise, be said of himself; and also that noble Earl, the Earl of Bedford, Generall of the horse, for both of them rode all day, being in the heads of the severall Troops and Regiments to give their directions, and to bring them on upon the enemy, hazarding their persons as far and further than any particular Souldier in the Army.

By this time all the enemie's foot being dispersed and gone excepting two Regiments, they retiring themselves, found their Ordnance behind them without any Guard, and there they made a stand, and made use of their Cannon, shooting divers shot at us; at which time our Regiment of foot began to want Powder, otherwise we had charged them both with horse and foot, which in all probability would have utterly ruined their Infantry, for those two Regiments were the onely stake which they had now left in the hedge: But partly through want of Ammunition, and partly being tyred with fighting all the day (the whole brunt of the Battle having been sustained by two Regiments of horse, and four or five of foot) we made no great haste to charge them, so that the enemies horse that had

been pillaging at Keynton had leisure to come about, some on one hand of us, and some on the other, and so joyned with their foot: Yet as they came back on our left hand, Sir Philip Stapleton, with his Troop, went out to charge some 4 or 5 Troops of them which went away from him as fast as they could upon the spur to the rest of their Company, and their foot that stood by their Ordnance, most of the enemie's horse being gathered to their foot, most of our horse also gathered to our foot, and so we stood horse and foot one against the other till it was night.
Our Army being thus possessed of the ground that the enemy chose to fight upon, stood there all night; the enemy having withdrawn their Army to the top of the hill for more security to themselves, where they made great fires all the night long, whilst we in the meantime drew backe some of our owne Ordnance, which they had once in their possession, and some of their's which they had left behinde.

The next morning, a little before it was light, we drew back our Army towards the Town to our other Brigadoe and Artillery and Ammunition that was come and lodged there, and the enemy drew out their horse in the morning upon the side of the hill, where staying till towards night, whil'st the foot were retyring behinde the hill and marching away, at length a little before night, their horse also marched away; and about an houre after, our horse also marched towards their Quarters, the Foot and some horse staying all night in their Quarters, in and before Keynton; and the next day the whole Army both horse and foot marched towards Warwicke to refresh themselves; instead of which, if they had marched towards Banbury, they would have found more victuals, and had in all probabilities dispersed all the foot of the King's Army, and taken his Canon and Carriages and sent his horse farther off to plunder, whereas now because we did not follow them though they quitted the field to us which we fought on and left their quarter before us the next day, yet they begin to question who had the day: It is true, there were Colours and Canon taken on both sides, without any great difference in the numbers, but for the number and quality of men slaine and hurt, it is verily believed, they left foure times as many at the least as we did, and in saying foure times as many, I am confident I speake much below the truth.
There were slaine on their side the Earl of Lindsey Generall of their Army, the Lord Aubigney, brother to the Duke of Richmond, Sir Edward Verny Colonell, John Monroe and divers other gentlemen and Commanders, and very many hurt. Of our side were slaine the Lord St. John, Colonell Charles Essex, Lieutenant Colonell Ramsey and none other of note, either killed or dangerously hurt that I can heare of; They acknowledge that they lost 1200 men, but it is thought they lost 2000: and whereas they report we lost divers thousands, where one man judgeth that we lost 400, ten men are of opinion that we lost not 200 Souldiers, besides the poore Waggoners and Carters.
These persons underwritten were all of the Right wing and never stirred from their Troops but they and their Troops fought till the last minute.

The Lord Generall's Regiment Sir William Belfore's Regiment
Sir Philip Stapleton Sir William Belfore
Captain Draper Sergeant Major Hurrey
Sergeant Major Gunter Lord Grey
Lord Brookes Captain Nathaniell Fiennes
Captain Sheffield Sir Arthur Hasilrigge
Captain Temple Captain Longe
Captain Cromwell

▲ Portrait of Prince Rupert (1619-1682) 1st Duke of Cumberland and Count Palatine of the Rhin

A FULL AND TRUE RELATION *of the great Battell fought between the King's Army, and his Excellency, the Earle of Essex, upon the 23 of October last past (being the same day twelve-moneth that the Rebellion broke out in Ireland) sent in a Letter from Captain Edward Kightley, now in the Army, to his friend Mr. Charles Lathum in Lumbard Street, London,*

Wherein may bee clearly seene what reason the Cavaliers have to give thankes for the Victory which they had over the Parliaments Forces. Judges 5-31.

"So let all thine enemies perish O Lord, but let them that love him, be as the Sun when he goeth forth in his might."

London: Printed November the 4, 1642.

Loving Cousin, I shall make so neare as I can a true, though long relation of the battell fought betweene the King's Army and our Army, under the conduct and command of my Lord Generall on Saturday October 22.

Our Forces were quartered very late and did lie remote one from the other, and my Lord Generall did quarter in a small Village where this Battell was fought, in a field called Great Kings Field, taking the name from a Battell there fought by King John as they say: on Sunday the 23 of October about one of the clocke in the afternoon, the Battell did begin and it continued untill it was very darke, the field was very great and large, and the King's Forces came down a great and long hill, he had the advantage of the ground and wind, and they did give a very brave charge, and did fight very valiantly: they were 15 Regiments of Foot and 60 Regiments of Horse, our Horse were under 40 Regiments and our Foot 11 Regiments: my Lord Generall did give the first charge, pressing them with 2 pieces of Ordnance which killed many of their men, and then the enemy did shoote one to us, which fell 20 yards short in a plowed Land, and did no harme, our Souldiers did many of them run away to wit blew Coats and Grey Coats, being two Regiments, and there did runne away, 600 horse, I was quartered five miles from the place, and heard not anything of it, until one of the clocke in the afternoone.

I halted thither with Sergent Major Duglis' troope, and over-tooke one other troope, and when I was entiring into the field, I thinke 200 horse came by me with all the speed they could out from the battell, saying, that the King had the victory, and that every man cried for God and King Charles.

I entreated, prayed and persuaded them to stay, and draw up in a body with our Troopes, for we saw them fighting, and the Field was not lost, but no perswasions would serve, and then I turning to our three troopes, two of them were runne away, and of my Troope I had not six and thirtie men left, but they were likewise runne away, I stayed with those men I had, being in a little field, and there was a way through, and divers of the enemy did runne that way both horse and foote.

I tooke away about tenne or twelve horse, swords, and armour, I could have killed 40 of the enemy, I let them passe disarming them, and giving the spoile to my Troopers; the Armies were both in a confusion, and I could not fall to them with out apparent loss of my selfe and those which were with me, the powder which the Enemy had was blowne up in the field, the Enemy ran away as well as our men, God did give the victory to us, there are but three men of note slain of ours, namely my Lord Saint John, Collonell Essex, and one other Captaine, whose name I have forgot. Captaine Fleming is either slaine or taken prisoner, and his Cornet, he had not one Officer which was a souldier, his Waggon and money is lost, and divers of the Captaines money and Waggons are lost, to great value, our foote and Dragooners were the greatest Pillagers, wee had the King's Standard one houre and a halfe, and after lost it againe: Wee did lose not above three hundred men, the enemy killed the Waggoners, women and little boyes of twelve years of age, we tooke seventeene Colours and five pieces of Ordnance, I believe there were not lesse than three thousand of the enemy slaine, for they lay on their own ground, twenty, and thirty of heapes together, the King did lose Lords, and a very

▲ Clash of cavalry in the battle.

great many of Gentlemen, but the certaine number of the slaine cannot bee knowne, we did take my Lord of Lindsey, Generall of the Foote, being shot in the thigh, who dyed the Tuesday morning following, and his body is sent away to be buryed, the Lo: Willoughby his son was taken, Lunsford, Vavasour, and others, being prisoners in Warwick Castle; on Munday there did runne from the King's Army 3000, foote in 40, 50, and 60 in Companies, wee kept the field all Sunday night, and all Munday, and then marched to our quarters, and on Munday the enemy would have given us another charge, but they could not get the foote to fight, notwithstanding they did beate them like dogs, this last Relation of the enemy I received from one which was a prisoner and got away. Banbury is taken by the King, there was 1000 Foote in it, the Captaines did run away, and the souldiers did deliver the Toune up without discharging one Musket. It was God's wonderful worke that we had the victory, we expect to march after the King.

The day after the Battell all our Forces, horse and foote were marched up, and other forces from remote parts, to the number of 5000, horse and foote more than were at the Battell, now at my writing, my Lord Generall is at Warwick, upon our next marching we doe expect another Battell, we here thinke that the King cannot strengthen himself, for the souldiers did still runne daily from him, and I believe if we come to fight a great part of them will never come up to the charge.

The King's guard were gentlemen of good quality, and I heard it, that there was not above 40 of them which returned out of the field, this is all I shall trouble you with, what is more, you will receive it from a better hand than mine: Let us pray one for another, God I hope will open the King's eyes, and send peace to our Kingdome.

I pray remember my love to all my friends; if I could write to them all I would, but for such newes I write you, impart it to them, my Leiutenant and I drinke to you all daily; all my runawayes, I stop their pay, some of them for two dayes some three dayes and some four dayes, which time they were gone from mee, and give their pay to the rest of the souldiers, two of my souldiers are runne away with their Horse and Armes: I rest, and commit you to God.

Your loving Cousin, EDWARD KIGHTLEY.

The Rebellion in Ireland and our Battell were both the 23 of October.

▲ Officer of Royalist cavalry in English civil war era.

APPENDIX

▲ English infantry officer 1644

THE NEW MODEL ARMY

THE NEW MODEL ARMY AND THE PRESBYTERIANS
From OLIVER CROMWELL by Samuel Rawson Gardiner, m.a. 1909

The New Model Army had been accepted by both Houses and by both parties in either House, because in no other way could the difficulties of the situation be met. The failure of the negotiations at Uxbridge had convinced the Presbyterians—at least for the moment—that Charles would give no help towards the settlement of the nation on any basis that their narrow minds could recognise as acceptable, and if the war was to be continued, what prospect was there of success under the old conditions? Nevertheless, the creation of the New Model was, in the main, Cromwell's work. Men are led by their passions more than by their reason, and if Cromwell had continued his invectives against Manchester, he would have roused an opposition which would have left little chance of the realisation of the hopes which he cherished most deeply in his heart. All through the discussion he had shown not only a readiness to sacrifice his own personal interests, but a determination to avoid even criticism of the actions of his opponents in all matters of less importance, provided that he had his way in the one thing most important of all.

Without a word of censure he had left the Presbyterians not only to negotiate with Charles, but to pass votes for the establishment of intolerant Presbyterianism in England. The skill with which he avoided friction by keeping himself in the background, whilst he allowed others to work for him, doubtless contributed much to his success. It revealed the highest qualities of statesmanship on the hypothesis that he was acting with a single eye to the public good. It revealed the lowest arts of the trickster, on the hypothesis that he was scheming for his own ultimate advantage. As human nature is constituted, there would be many who would convince themselves that the lower interpretation of his conduct was the true one.

At all events, the New Model Army was being brought into shape in the spring of 1645. It was composed partly of men pressed into the service, partly of soldiers who had served in former armies. That the Puritan, and even the Independent element, was well represented amongst the cavalry of which Cromwell's troops formed the nucleus, there can be little doubt; and even amongst the infantry, the fact that it could only be recruited from those parts of England which at that time acknowledged the authority of the Houses, and that in those counties Puritanism was especially rife, would naturally introduce into the ranks a considerable number of Puritans, whether Independent or not. The army, however, was certainly not formed on the principles which had guided Cromwell in the selection of his first troopers, and indeed it was impossible to select 30,000 men on the exclusive plan which had been found possible in the enlistment of a single troop or a single regiment. What chiefly—so far as the rank and file were concerned—distinguished the New Model from preceding armies was that it was regularly paid. Hitherto the soldiers had been dependent on intermittent Parliamentary grants, or still more intermittent efforts of local committees. All this was now to be changed.

A regular taxation was assessed on the counties for the support of the new army, and the constant pay thus secured was likely to put an end to the desertions on a large scale which had afflicted former commanders, thus rendering it possible to bring the new force under rigorous discipline, a discipline which punished even more severely offences against morality than those directed against military efficiency.

The higher the state of discipline the more important is the selection of officers; and here at least Cromwell's views had full scope. On the mere ground that it was desirable to place command in the hands of those who were most strenuous in the prosecution of the war, the preference was certain to be given to men who were least hampered by a desire to make terms with an unbeaten King—in other words, to Independents rather than to Presbyterians. In another way Cromwell's ideas were carried out. "I had rather," he had once said, "have a plain russet-coated captain that knows what he fights for, and loves what he knows, than that which you call a gentleman and nothing else. I honour a gentleman that is so indeed." There was no distinction of social rank amongst the officers of the New Model. Amongst them were men of old families such as Fairfax and Montague, side by side with Hewson, the cobbler, and Pride, the drayman. If ever the army should be drawn within the circle of politics, much would follow from the adoption of a system of promotion which grounded itself on military efficiency alone.

For the present the services of the new army were required solely in the field. On April 20 Cromwell, who was permitted to retain his commission forty days after the ordinance had passed, and whose allotted term had not yet expired, was sent with his cavalry to sweep round the King's head-quarters at Oxford in order to break up his arrangements for sending out the artillery needed by Rupert if he was again to take the field. Cromwell's movement was completely successful. He not only scattered a Royalist force at Islip, and captured Blechington House by sheer bluff, but he swept up all the draught horses on which Charles had counted for the removal of the guns, andthus incapacitated the enemy from immediate action. Rupert had to wait patiently for some time before he could leave his quarters.

It is seldom that men realise at first the necessary consequences of an important change, and, on this occasion, the Committee of Both Kingdoms and the Parliament itself were slow to discover that, if the new army was to achieve victory, its movements must be guided, not by politicians at Westminster, but by the general in the field. The first act of the Committee was to send Fairfax with eleven thousand men to the relief of Taunton, where Blake, who not long before had defended Lyme against all the efforts of the Royalists to take it, was now holding out to the last with scanty protection from the fortifications he had improvised.

The Committee's orders, necessary perhaps at first, were persisted in even after it was known that Charles had been joined at Oxford by the field army which had hitherto protected the besiegers of Taunton in the West, and that, whilst a much smaller force than eleven thousand men would be now sufficient to raise the siege, every soldier that could be spared was needed farther east. The next blunder of the Committee was even worse. Charles had marched to the North with all the force he could gather, in the hope of undoing the consequences of Marston Moor. If there was one lesson which the Committee ought to have learnt from the campaign of the preceding year it was that it is useless to besiege towns whilst the enemy's army remains unbeaten in the field. Yet when every military consideration spoke with no uncertain voice for the policy of following up Charles's army without remission till it had been defeated, the sage Committee-men at Westminster ordered Fairfax to besiege Oxford. Charles, at liberty to direct his movements where he would, had been deflected from his course, and on May 31 had stormed Leicester.

The news shook the Committee's resolution to keep the direction of the army in its own feeble hands. On June 2 it directed Fairfax to break up the siege of Oxford. On the 4th a petition from the London Common Council asked that, though the forty days during which Cromwell kept his appointment under the Self-Denying Ordinance had now elapsed, he might be placed at the head of a new army to be raised in the Eastern Association. Another petition from Fairfax's officers asked that he might be placed in the vacant lieutenant-generalship. The Commons agreed, but, for the present at least, the Lords withheld their consent.

At a later time, when events had rendered refusal impossible, the Lords gave their consent to an appointment for which Cromwell was certainly not disqualified by anything in the Self-Denying Ordinance in the form in which they had allowed it to pass; considering that that Ordinance merely demanded the surrender of his commission, without imposing any bar to his reappointment.

When on June 14 the army under Fairfax found itself in presence of the King at Naseby, Cromwell was once more in command of the horse. As usual in those days the infantry was in the centre. On the two wings were the cavalry, that on the right under Cromwell in person, that on the left under Ireton. Ireton was driven back by Rupert, who, having learned nothing since his headlong charge at Edgehill, dashed in pursuit without a moment's thought for the fortunes of the remainder of the King's army. Cromwell, after driving off the horse opposed to him, drew rein, as he had done at Marston Moor, to watch the sway of the battle he had left behind him. Seeing his duty clear, he left three regiments to continue the pursuit, and with the remainder fell upon the Royalist infantry, and with the help of Fairfax's own foot destroyed or captured the whole body.

Rupert returned too late to do anything but join Charles in his flight. Five thousand prisoners had been taken, of whom no less than five hundred were officers, while Charles's whole train of artillery remained in the hands of the victors. That Cromwell had contributed more than any other man to this crushing victory was beyond dispute.

Cromwell, as was his usual habit, ascribed this success to Divine aid. "I can say this of Naseby," he wrote, "that when I saw the enemy draw up and march in gallant order towards us, and we a company of poor ignorant men to seek to order our battle, the General having commanded me to order all the horse, I could not—riding alone about my business—but smile out to God praises in assurance of victory, because God would, by things that are not, bring to naught things that are, of which I had great assurance—and God did it." No doubt, as has been said, Cromwell omitted to mention that the Parliamentary army had numbers on its side—not much less than 14,000, opposed to 7,500. But it was not the numerical superiority of the Parliamentarians which won the day. It did not enable Ireton to withstand Rupert, and the infantry in the centre was already giving way when Cromwell returned to assist it. It was the discipline rather than the numbers of Cromwell's horse aided by the superb generalship of their commander that gained the day. Cromwell, when he wrote of his soldiers as 'poor ignorant men,' was doubtless glancing back in thought at his own early criticism of the fugitives at Edgehill. The yeomen and peasants whom he had gathered round him owed much to discipline and leadership; but they owed much also to the belief embedded in their hearts that they were fighting in the cause of God.

After the victory at Naseby the issue of the struggle was practically decided. There was another fight at Langport, where Fairfax defeated a force with which Goring attempted to guard the western counties; but after this the war resolved itself into a succession of sieges which could end but in one way as Charles had no longer a field army to bring to the relief of Royalist garrisons. For some months Cromwell, sometimes in combination with Fairfax, sometimes in temporary command of a separate force, was untiring in the energy which he threw into his work. Charles was full of combinations which never resulted in practical advantage to his cause. At one time his hopes were set upon Montrose, who, after his brilliant victories, expected to bring an army of Highlanders to aid of the royal cause. At another time he looked with equal hopefulness to Glamorgan, who was to conduct an Irish army to England. Montrose's scheme was wrecked at Philiphaugh, and Glamorgan's concessions to the Irish Catholics were divulged and had to be disavowed. On March 31, 1646 Sir Jacob Astley bringing 3,000 men, the last Royalist force in existence, to the relief of Charles at Oxford, was forced to surrender at Stow-on-the-Wold. "You have done your work," said the veteran to his captors, "and may go play, unless you will fall out among yourselves." Though Oxford and Newark were still untaken, the end of the war was now a mere question of days.

"Honest men," wrote Cromwell to Speaker Lenthall soon after the victory of Naseby "served you faithfully in this action. Sir, they are trusty—I beseech you in the name of God, not to discourage them—I wish this action may beget thankfulness and humility in all that are concerned in it. He that ventures his life for the liberty of his country, I wish he trust God for the liberty of his conscience, and you for the liberty he fights for." "All this," he continued three months later, in the same strain, after the storm of Bristol, "is none other than the work of God; he must be a very atheist that doth not acknowledge it. It may be thought that some praises are due to those gallant men of whose valour so much mention is made:—Their humble suit to you and all that have an interest in this blessing is that, in the remembrance of God's praises, they may be forgotten.

It's their joy that they are instruments of God's glory and their country's good. It's their honour that God vouchsafes to use them.... Sir, they that have been employed in this service know that faith and prayer obtained this city for you: I do not say ours only, but of the people of God with you and all England over, who have wrestled with God for a blessing in this very thing. Our desires are that God may be glorified by the same spirit of faith by which we ask all our sufficiency and have received it. It is meet that He have all the praise. Presbyterians, Independents, all had here the same spirit of faith and prayer, the same presence and answer; they agree here, know no names of difference; pity it is it should be otherwise anywhere! All that believe have the real unity which is most glorious because inward and spiritual in the Body and to the Head. As for being united in forms, commonly called uniformity, every Christian will, for peace sake, study and do as far as conscience will permit. And from brethren, in things of the mind, we look for no compulsion but that of light and reason. In other things, God hath put the sword in the Parliament's hands for the terror of evil-doers and the praises of them that do well. If any plead exemption from that, he knows not the Gospel; if any would wring that out of your hands, or steal it from you, under what pretence soever, I hope they shall do it without effect."

No words can better depict the state of Cromwell's mind at this time. Of the religion to which the King and his followers clung there is no question in his thoughts. He would be unwilling to listen to the suggestion that it was to be counted as religion in any worthy sense. Parliament, mutilated as it was, is the authority ordained by God to keep order in the land. For that very reason Parliament was bound to allow full liberty to God's children, whatever might be their differences on matters of discipline or practice. Within the limits

▲ English infantry pikeman 1645

of Puritanism, no intolerance might be admitted. A common spiritual emotion—not external discipline or intellectual agreement—was the test of brotherhood. So resolved was the House of Commons to discountenance this view of the case, that in ordering the publication of Cromwell's two despatches, it mutilated both of them by the omission of the passages advocating liberty of conscience.

At the present day we are inclined to blame Cromwell, not for going too far in the direction of toleration, but for not going far enough. In the middle of the seventeenth century the very idea of toleration in any shape was peculiar to a chosen few. That the majority of the Puritan clergy were bitterly opposed to it affords no matter for surprise. As men of some education and learning, and with a professional confidence in the certainty of their own opinions, they looked with contempt not merely on views different from their own, but also on the persons who, often without the slightest mental culture, ventured to produce out of the Bible schemes of doctrine sometimes immoral, and very often—at least in the opinions of the Presbyterian divines—blasphemous and profane. Even where this was not the case, there remained the danger of seeing the Church of England—which was held to have been purified by the abolition of episcopacy and the banishment of the ceremonies favoured by the bishops—degenerate into a chaos in which a thousand sects battled for their respective creeds, instead of meekly accepting the gospel dealt out to them by their well-instructed pastors. Richard Baxter was a favourable specimen of the Presbyterian clergy.

Conciliatory in temper, he was yet an ardent controversialist, and, for a few months after the battle of Naseby, he accepted the position of chaplain to Whalley's regiment, with the avowed intention of persuading the sectaries to abandon their evil ways. He soon discovered that the greater part of the infantry of the New Model Army was by no means sectarian or even Puritan in its opinions. "The greatest part of the common soldiers," he wrote, "especially of the foot, were ignorant men of little religion, abundance of them such as had been taken prisoners or turned out of garrisons under the King, and had been soldiers in his army; and these would do anything to please their officers." In other words, the sectarian officers could command the services of the army as a whole, backed as they would be by the most energetic of the private soldiers.

Nor was Baxter longer in discovering that the military preachers were ready to question received doctrine in politics as well as in religion. "I perceived," he declared, "they took the King for a tyrant and an enemy, and really intended to master him, and they thought if they might fight against him they might kill or conquer him, and if they might conquer they were never more to trust him further than he was in their power; and that they thought it folly to irritate him either by wars or contradictions in Parliament, if so be they must needs take him for their King, and trust him with their lives when they had thus displeased him." These audacious reasoners went further still. "What," they asked, "were the Lords of England but William the Conqueror's colonels, or the Barons but his majors, or the Knights but his captains?" "They plainly showed me," complained Baxter, "that they thought God's providence would cast the trust of religion and the Kingdom upon them as conquerors; they made nothing of all the most wise and godly in the armies and garrisons that were not of their way. *Per fas aut nefas*, by law or without it, they were resolved to take down not only Bishops and liturgy and ceremonies, but all that did withstand their way. They ... most honoured the Separatists, Anabaptists and Antinomians; but Cromwell and his council took on them to join themselves to no party, but to be for the liberty of all."

'To be for the liberty of all' was recognised as being Cromwell's position. There is every reason to suppose that he had at this time little sympathy with the aspirations of those who would have made the army the lever wherewith to obtain political results otherwise unobtainable. In his Bristol despatch he had pointedly adhered to the doctrine that the sword had been placed by God in the hands of Parliament, and for the present he was inclined to look to Parliament alone for the boon he asked of it. What makes Cromwell's biography so interesting is his perpetual effort to walk in the paths of legality—an effort always frustrated by the necessities of the situation.

It is difficult for us, nursled as we are under a regime of religious liberty, to understand how hateful Cromwell's proposal was in the eyes of the vast majority of his contemporaries. Not only did it shock those who looked down with scorn on the vagaries of the tub-preacher, but it aroused fears lest religious sectarianism should, by splitting up the nation into hostile parties, lead the way to political weakness.

To every nation it is needful that there be some bond of common emotion which shall enable it to present an undivided front against its enemies, and such a bond was more than ever needful at a time when loyalty to the throne had been suspended. It was Cromwell's merit to have seen that this bond would be strengthened, not weakened, by the permission of divergencies in teaching and practice, so long as there was agreement on the main grounds of spiritual Puritanism. If on the one hand he was behind Roger Williams in theoretical conception, he was in advance of him in his attempt to fit in his doctrines with the practical needs of his time. Some assistance Cromwell had from men with whom, on other grounds, he had little sympathy.

The Westminster Assembly of divines, which had been sitting since 1643, had done its best to impose the Presbyterian system on England, but in the House of Commons there was a small group of Erastian lawyers, with the learned Selden at their head, which was strong enough to carry Parliament with it in resistance to the imposition upon England of a Scottish Presbyterianism—that is to say, of an ecclesiastical system in which matters of religion were to be disposed of in the Church Courts without any appeal to the lay element in the State; though, on the other hand, it must not be forgotten that in those very Church Courts the lay element found its place. The Erastians, however, preferred to uphold the supreme authority of the laity represented in Parliament—as the lawyers of the preceding century had upheld the authority of the laity represented in the King—probably because they knew that the lay members of the Presbyterian assemblies were pretty sure to fall under the influence of the clergy. Selden indeed was no admirer of the enthusiasms of the sects; but his cool, dispassionate way of treating their claims would, in the end, make for liberty even more certainly than the burning zeal of a Williams or a Cromwell.

With the surrender of Astley at Stow-on-the-Wold a new situation was created. The time had arrived to which Cromwell had looked forward after the second battle of Newbury, the time when Charles—no longer having any hope of dictating terms to his enemies—would probably be ready to accept some compromise which might give to Cromwell and the Independent party that religious freedom which the Presbyterians at Westminster found it so hard to concede. It did not need a tithe of Cromwell's sagacity to convince him that a settlement would have a far greater chance of proving durable if it were honestly accepted by the King than if it were not. Yet it did not augur well for a settlement that Charles, knowing that if he remained at Oxford a few weeks would see him a prisoner in the hands of the army, rode off towards Newark, which was at that time besieged by the Scots, and on May 5, 1646, gave himself up to the Scottish commander at Southwell. The Scots having extracted from him an order to the Governor of Newark to surrender the place, marched off, with him in their train, to Newcastle, where they would be the better able to maintain their position against any attack by the army of the English Parliament. If Charles expected to make the Scots his tools, he was soon undeceived. He was treated virtually as a prisoner under honourable restraint, and given to understand that he was expected to establish Presbyterianism in England.

A few days before Charles left Oxford, Cromwell had come up to Westminster to take part in the discussions on a settlement which were certain to follow on the close of the war. He saw his views better supported in the House of Commons than they had been when he was last within its walls. A series of elections had taken place to fill the seats vacated by the expulsion of Royalists, and the majority of the recruiters—as the new members were called—were determined Independents, that is to say, favourers of religious liberty within the bounds of Puritanism. Amongst them were Ireton, who had commanded the left wing at Naseby, and who was soon to become Cromwell's son-in-law; Fleetwood, now a colonel in the New Model Army, Blake, the defender of Taunton, hereafter to be the great admiral of the Commonwealth and Protectorate, together with other notables of the army. Yet the Presbyterians still kept a majority in the House.

They had already, on March 14, secured the passing of an ordinance establishing Presbyterianism in England, though it was to differ from the Scottish system in that the Church was placed, in the last resort, under the supreme authority of Parliament. An English Presbyterian could not, even when we needed Scottish help, conform himself entirely to the Scottish model. It is true that the ordinance was only very partially carried out, but there can be little doubt that it would have been more generally obeyed if the negotiations, which the Parliamentary majority in accordance with the Scots were conducting with the King at Newcastle, had been attended with success.

That Cromwell watched these negotiations with the keenest interest may be taken for granted; but he does not seem to have had any opportunity, as a simple member of the House, for doing more. We can indeed only conjecture, though with tolerable certitude, that he was well pleased with the widening of the breach between the Presbyterians and the King, caused by the determination of Charles to make no stipulation which would lead to the abolition of episcopacy. Nor can he have been otherwise than well pleased when, on January 30, 1647, the Scottish soldiers, having received part of the sum due to them for their services in England with promise of the remainder, marched for Scotland, having first delivered Charles over to commissioners appointed by the English Parliament, who conducted him to Holmby House in Northamptonshire, which had been assigned to him by Parliament as a residence.

At last the time had arrived when a peaceful settlement of the distracted country appeared to have come in sight and, for the time at least, the Presbyterians seemed to have the strongest cards in their hands.

They had a majority in Parliament, and it was for them, therefore, to formulate the principles on which the future institutions of the country were to be built. That the country was with them in wishing, on the one hand, for an arrangement in which the King could reappear as a constitutional factor in the Government, and, on the other hand, for a total or partial disbandment of the army and a consequent relief from taxation, can hardly be denied. The great weakness,and, as it proved, the insuperable weakness of the Presbyterians lay in the incapacity of their leaders to understand the characters of the men with whom they had to deal. Right as they were in their opinion that the nation would readily accept a constitutional monarchy, it was impossible to persuade them, as was really the case, that Charles would never willingly submit to be bound by the limitations of constitutional monarchy, and still less to allow, longer than he could possibly help, the Church to be modelled after any kind of Presbyterian system. That he had the strongest possible conviction on religious grounds that episcopacy was of Divine ordinance is beyond doubt, and on this point his tenacious, though irresolute, mind was strengthened by an assurance that in fighting in the cause of the bishops he was really fighting in the cause of God. Yet the controversy had a political as well as a religious side.

In Scotland Presbyterianism meant the predominance of the clergy. In England it would mean the predominance of the country nobility and gentry, who, either in their private capacity or collectively in Parliament, presented to benefices, and in Parliament kept the final control over the Church in their own hands. Episcopacy, on the other hand, meant that the control over the Church was in the hands of men appointed by the King.

The folly of the Presbyterians appeared, not in their maintenance of their own views, but in their fancying that if they could only persuade Charles to agree to give them their way temporarily, they would have done sufficient to gain their cause. Early in 1647 they proposed that Presbyterianism should be established in England for three years, and that the militia should remain in the power of Parliament for ten.

They could not see that at the end of the periods fixed Charles would have the immense advantage of finding himself face to face with a system which had ceased to have any legal sanction. Common prudence suggested that whatever settlement was arrived at it should, at least, have in favour of its continuance the presumption of permanency accorded to every established institution which is expected to remain in possession of the field till definite steps are taken for its abolition.

It is possible indeed that the Presbyterians calculated on the unpopularity of episcopacy and of all that episcopacy was likely to bring with it. It is true that not even an approximate estimate can be given of the numerical strength of ecclesiastical parties. No religious census was taken, and there is every reason to believe that, if it had been taken, it would have failed to convey any accurate information.

There is little doubt that very considerable numbers, probably much more than a bare majority of the population, either did not care for ecclesiastical disputes at all, or at least did not care for them sufficiently to offer armed resistance to any form of Church-Government or Church-teaching likely to be established either by Parliament or by King. Yet all the evidence we possess shows the entire absence of any popular desire amongst the laity outside the families of the Royalist gentry and their immediate dependants to bring back either episcopacy or the Prayer Book. Riots there occasionally were, but these were riots because amusements had been stopped, and especially because the jollity of Christmas was forbidden; not because the service in church was conducted in one way or another. It is sometimes forgotten that the Puritan or semi-Puritan clergy had a strong hold upon the Church down to the days of Laud, and that the Calvinistic teaching which had been in favour even with the bishops towards the close of the reign of Elizabeth had been widely spread down to the same time, so that the episcopalians could not count on that resistance to organic change which would certainly have sprung up if the Laudian enforcement of discipline had continued for seventy years instead of seven.

Whilst episcopacy found its main support in the King, the sects found their main support in the army, and

Parliament at once fell in with the popular demand for weakening the army. Before February was over, it had resolved that 6,600 horse and dragoons should be retained in England, but that, except the men needed for a few garrisons, none of the infantry of the New Model Army should be kept in the service.

Their place was to be supplied by a militia which, consisting as it did of civilians pursuing their usual avocations for the greater part of the year, and, except in times of invasion or rebellion, only called out for a few days' drill, would be most unlikely to join in any attempt to cross the wishes of Parliament.

Cavalry, moreover, being, in the long run, unable to act without the support of infantry, the 6,600 horse kept on foot would be powerless to impose a policy by force on the Parliament. As more than half of the infantry, whose services in England were no longer required, would be needed to carry on the war in Ireland, now almost entirely in the hands of the so-called rebels, it was thought that the number necessary for this purpose would volunteer for service in that country, and the rest be readily induced to return amongst the civilian population out of which they had sprung.

Having thus, in imagination, weakened the army as a whole, the Presbyterian majority proceeded to deal with the officers of the cavalry destined for service in England. Retaining Fairfax as Commander-in-Chief, they voted that no officer should serve under him who refused to take the Covenant, and to conform to the Church-government established by Parliament. They also voted that, with the exception of Fairfax, no officer should hold a higher rank than that of colonel; in other words, they pronounced the dismissal of Lieutenant-General Cromwell from the service. It was characteristic of Cromwell that in a letter written by him to Fairfax his personal grievance finds no place. "Never," he writes, "were the spirits of men more embittered than now. Surely the Devil hath but a short time. Upon the Fast-day," he adds in a postscript, "divers soldiers were raised, as I heard, both horse and foot—near two hundred in Covent Garden—to prevent us soldiers from cutting the Presbyterians' throats! These are fine tricks to mock God with." Yet, irritated as he was, he gave no sign of any thought of resistance. "In the presence of Almighty God, before whom I stand," he declared to the House, "I know the army will disband and lay down their arms at your door whenever you will command them." His own dismissal he took calmly. Towards the end of March he was in frequent conference with the Elector Palatine who had offered him a command in Germany, where the miserable Thirty Years' War was still dragging on, and where the cause of toleration, apparently lost in England, might possibly be served.

C This is Carlyle's reading, but the original manuscript is torn, and what indications there are show that the words cannot be 'us soldiers'. But I have no emendation to suggest.

The Presbyterian leaders, Holles, Stapleton, Maynard, and the rest of them, must have flattered themselves that they were at last in the full career of success. To have Cromwell's word for it that the army would accept disbandment, and to see the back of the man whom they most feared, was a double stroke of fortune on which they could hardly have calculated. In their delight at the good fortune which had fallen into their laps, they forgot, in the first place, that there were many officers, besides Cromwell, who mistrusted their policy; and in the second place that, if these officers were to be deprived of their influence over the private soldiers, care must be taken to leave no material grievance of the latter unrelieved.

On March 21 and 22 a deputation from Parliament which met forty-three officers in Saffron Walden Church was told that no one present would volunteer for Ireland unless a satisfactory answer were given to four questions: What regiments were to be kept up in England? Who was to command in Ireland? What was to be the assurance for the pay and maintenance of the troops going to Ireland? Finally, what was to be done to secure the arrears due to the men and indemnity for military actions in the past war which a civil court might construe into robbery and murder? In addition to these demands, a petition was drawn up in the name of the soldiers, asking for various concessions, of which the principal ones concerned the arrears and the indemnity. If the Presbyterian leaders had been possessed of a grain of common sense, they would have seen that they could not retain the submission of an army and be oblivious of its material interests.

As it was, they treated the action of the soldiers as mere mutiny, summoned the leading officers to the bar, and declared all who supported the petition to be enemies of the State and disturbers of the peace.

Cromwell's position was one of great difficulty. As a soldier and a man of order, he abhorred any semblance of mutiny, and he had shown by his readiness to accept a command in Germany that he had no wish to redress the balance of political forces by throwing his sword into the scale; but it did not need his distrust of the political capacity of the Presbyterian leaders to help him to the conclusion that they were wholly in the wrong

▲ A tale of Edgehill after John Seymour-Lucas

in their method of dealing with the army. It was not a case in which soldiers refused to obey the commands of their superiors in accordance with the terms of their enlistment. They were asked to undertake new duties, and in the case of those who were expected to betake themselves to Ireland, actually to volunteer for a new service, and yet, forsooth, they were to be treated as mutineers, because they asked for satisfaction in their righteous claims.

Cromwell, even if he had wished to oppose the army to the Parliament, would have had nothing to do but to sit still, whilst his opponents accumulated blunder after blunder. The House of Commons being unable to extract any signs of yielding from the officers whom it had summoned to the bar, sent them back to their posts. It then appointed Skippon, a good disciplinarian, of no special repute as a general, to command in Ireland; after which, without offering in any way to meet the soldiers' demands, it sent a new body of commissioners, amongst whom was Sir William Waller, a stout adherent of the Presbyterian cause, to urge on the formation of a new army for Ireland. The commissioners, on their arrival at Saffron Walden, were not slow in discovering that the officers did not take kindly to the idea of Skippon's command. "Fairfax and Cromwell," they shouted, "and we all go." The commissioners gained the promise of a certain number of officers and soldiers to go to Ireland; but, on the whole, their mission was a failure.

They had not been empowered to offer payment of arrears, and, as they ought to have foreseen, the indignation of the large number of soldiers who complained that they were being cheated of their pay, threw power into the hands of the minority, known as the "Godly party," which held forth the doctrine that, now that Parliament was shrinking from the fulfilment of its duty, it was time for the army to step forward as a political power, and to secure the settlement of the nation on the basis of civil and religious liberty. The idea was also entertained that it would be easier for the army than it had been for Parliament to come to terms with the King, and that it was for the soldiers to fetch him from Holmby and to replace him, on fair conditions, on the throne.

Of Cromwell's feelings during these weeks we have little evidence. From the house which, since the preceding year, he had occupied with his family in Drury Lane, he watched events, without attempting to modify them. In the latter part of April both he and Vane, who was now his fast friend, with a tie cemented by a common interest in religious liberty, absented themselves, save on a few rare occasions, from the sittings of Parliament. The incalculable stupidity of the Presbyterian leaders must have made Cromwell more than ever doubtful of the possibility of getting from them a remedy for the evils of the nation. By the end of April it was known that only 2,320 soldiers had volunteered for Ireland. Then, and not till then, Parliament came to the conclusion that something ought to be done about the arrears, and ordered that six weeks' pay should be offered to every disbanded soldier. It was a mere fraction of what was due, and a soldier need not be abnormally suspicious to come to the conclusion that, when once he had left the ranks, his prospect of getting satisfaction for the remainder of his claim was exceedingly slight. Thus driven to the wall, eight of the cavalry regiments chose, each of them, two Agitators, or, as in modern speech they would be styled, Agents, to represent them in the impending negotiation for their rights, and the sixteen thus chosen drew up letters to the Generals, Fairfax, Cromwell, Ireton and Skippon.

As the cavalry was the most distinctively political portion of the army, the writers of these letters for the first time stepped beyond the bounds of material grievance, complaining of a design to break and ruin the army, and of the intention of 'some who had lately tasted of sovereignty to become masters and degenerate into tyrants'. The House, beyond measure indignant, summoned to the bar three of the Agitators who brought the letters to Westminster; but on their refusal to answer questions put to them without order from their military constituents, sent Cromwell, Ireton and Skippon to assure the soldiers that they should have the indemnity they craved, together with a considerable part of their arrears and debentures for the rest.

There is no reason to doubt that Cromwell sympathised with the soldiers in their desire for a just settlement of their claims, whilst he was still disinclined to support them in their design of gaining influence over the Government. When he reached Saffron Walden he found that the infantry regiments had followed the example of the cavalry, and that a body of Agitators had been chosen to represent the whole army.

The result of their conferences with the officers was the production of *A Declaration of the Army*, drawn up on May 16, with which Cromwell appears to have been entirely satisfied, as, while it insisted on a redress of practical grievances, it contained no claim to political influence. If the Houses had frankly accepted the situation, Cromwell and his colleagues would have succeeded in averting, at least for a time, the danger of investing the army with political power.

On his return Cromwell found signs that the Parliamentary majority was even less inclined to do justice to the soldiers than when he had left Westminster. During his absence, Parliamentary authority to discipline and train the militia of the City had been given to a committee named by the Common Council of London. The Common Council was a Presbyterian body, and its committee proceeded to eject every officer tainted with Independency. The city militia numbered 18,000 men, and it looked as if the majority in Parliament was preparing a force which might be the nucleus of an army to be opposed to the soldiers of Fairfax and Cromwell. In Scotland, too, there was an army of more than 6,000 men, under the command of David Leslie—no inconsiderable general—which might perhaps be brought to the help of the Parliament against its own soldiers, as Leven's army had, three years before, been brought to its assistance against the King. Charles, too, on May 12—Cromwell being still absent from Westminster—had at last replied to the proposals made to him early in the year, and had offered to concede the militia for ten years, and a Presbyterian establishment for three, the clergy being allowed to discuss in the meanwhile the terms of a permanent settlement. In the very probable event of their disagreeing, it would be easy for Charles, at the end of the three years, to contend that episcopacy was again the legal government of the Church—especially as he was at once to return to Westminster, where he would be able to exercise all the influence which would again be at his command. On May 18 this offer was however accepted by the English Presbyterians, as well as by the Scottish Commissioners, as a fair basis of an understanding with the King.

No wonder that the soldiers took alarm, or that on the 19th the Agitators issued an appeal to the whole army to hang together in resistance.

Nevertheless, when Cromwell reappeared in the House on May 21, and read out the joint report of the deputation, he was able to declare his belief that the army would disband, though it would refuse to volunteer for Ireland. At first the House seemed ready to take the reasonable course, approving of an ordinance granting the required indemnity, and favourably considering another to provide a real and visible security for so much of the arrears as was left unpaid. At the same time the arrears to be given in hand were raised from the pay of six weeks to that of eight. Yet whatever the Presbyterians might offer, they were unable to trust the army, and on the 23rd they discussed with Lauderdale, who was in England as a Scottish member of the Committee of Both Kingdoms, and Bellièvre, who was the Ambassador of the King of France, a scheme for bringing a Scottish army into England. Talk about securing the King's person, which had prevailed in some regiments a short time before, had come to their ears, and furnished them with the excuse that they were but anticipating their opponents. They accordingly proposed to counteract this design by removing Charles either to some English town, or even to Scotland. Their hopes of being able to carry out this daring project were the higher as Colonel Graves, who commanded the guard at Holmby, was himself a Presbyterian on whom they could depend to carry out their instructions.

Though nothing was absolutely settled, the conduct of the House of Commons reflected the policy of its leaders. It dropped its consideration of the ordinance assigning security for the soldiers' arrears and resolved to proceed at once to disband the army, beginning on June 1.

The announcement of this resolution brought consternation to those who were doing their best to keep the soldiers within the bounds of obedience. "I doubt," wrote the author of a letter which was probably addressed by Ireton to his father-in-law, "the disobliging of so faithful an army will be repented of; provocation and exasperation make men think of what they never intended. They are possessed, as far as I can discern, with this opinion that if they be thus scornfully dealt with for their faithful services whilst the sword is in their hands, what shall their usage be when they are dissolved?" Two days later, another writer, speaking of the commissioners appointed by Parliament to disband the regiments, added the prophetic words: "They may as well send them among so many bears to take away their whelps". It was perfectly true.

When on June 1 the commissioners attempted to disband Fairfax's regiment at Chelmsford, it broke into mutiny and marched for Newmarket, where Fairfax had appointed a rendezvous to consider the situation.

It was not that the mass of the army had any inclination to interfere in politics. "Many of the soldiers," wrote the commissioners, "being dealt with, profess that money is the only thing they insist upon, and that four months' pay would have given satisfaction."

Such an event could not but drive Cromwell to reconsider his position. Whether he liked it or not, the army had, through the bungling of the Presbyterian leaders, broken loose from the authority of Parliament. It was impossible for him to give his support to Parliament when it was about, with the aid of the Scottish army, to restore the King on terms which, whether the King or the Presbyterians gained the upper hand in the game of intrigue which was sure to follow, could only end in the destruction of that religious liberty for the sects which, though without legal sanction, had been gained as a matter of fact. Yet the alternative seemed to be the abandonment of the country to military anarchy, or if that were averted to the sway of the army over the State. Only one way of escape from the dilemma presented itself, and that way Cromwell seized.

Cromwell, it must once more be said, was no Republican or Parliamentary theorist. Parliament was to him mainly an authority under which he had fought for the great ends he had in view.

Now that it had sunk to be no more than a tool in the hands of politicians who, aiming at the establishment of an ecclesiastical despotism, could think of no better means wherewith to compass their evil ends than the rekindling of the conflagration of civil war with the aid of a Scottish army and of French diplomacy, and who had proved themselves bunglers in their own noxious work, it was necessary to look about for some fresh basis of authority, which would save England from the danger of falling under the sway of a Prætorian guard.

Nor was that basis far to seek. Cromwell had fought the King unsparingly—not to destroy him, but to reduce him to the acceptance of honourable terms. The terms which the Presbyterians had offered to Charles had not been honourable. They had demanded that he should proscribe his own religion and impose upon his subjects an ecclesiastical system which he believed to be hateful to God and man.

Was this to be the result of all the blood and treasure that had been expended? What if the King could be won to bring back peace and good government to the land by fairer treatment and by the restoration of his beneficent authority? The call for a restoration of the King to power did not arise merely from the monarchical theories of a few enthusiasts. It was deeply rooted in the consciousness of generations.

A few years before it had been inconceivable to Englishmen that order could be maintained without a king, and with the great mass of Englishmen this view was still prevalent. We can hardly go wrong if we suppose that Cromwell shared the hope that Charles, by more generous treatment than that which Parliament had

▲ English cavalry roundhead (parliamentary New Model Army)

accorded to him, would allow the chiefs of the army to mediate between him and Parliament, and consent to accept the restitution of so much of his authority as would safeguard the religious and political development of the country on the lines of reform rather than on those of revolution.

If this, or anything like this, was to be accomplished, the conjuncture would admit of no delay. In a few days—perhaps in a few hours—the plans of the Presbyterian leaders would be matured, and Charles would be spirited away from Holmby, either to be hurried off to Scotland, or to be placed under the care of the new Presbyterian militia in London. The commander of the guard at Holmby, Colonel Graves, was prepared to carry out any instructions which might reach him from his leaders at Westminster.

Not only this, but on May 31, the day before the meeting at Chelmsford, a Parliamentary committee had issued orders to seize the artillery of the army at Oxford, and thus to weaken its powers of action as a military force. The situation was one which, by the necessity of the case, must have occupied the attention of the Agitators, and though no certainty is to be reached, it is probable that it was with them that the plan adopted originated rather than with Cromwell. Again and again in the course of his career he will be found hanging back from decisive action involving a change of front in his political action, and there is every indication that, on this occasion too, he accepted—and that not without considerable hesitation—a design which had been formed by others.

Such hesitation, however, was with him perfectly consistent with the promptest and most determined action when the time for hesitation was at an end. On May 31, the day on which the order for seizing the artillery at Oxford was despatched from London, a meeting was held at Cromwell's house in Drury Lane, at which was present a certain Cornet Joyce, who had apparently been authorised by the Agitators to secure the artillery at Oxford, and then to proceed to Holmby to hinder the removal of the King by the Presbyterians, if not to carry him off to safer quarters.

For such an action as this the Agitators, as they well knew, had no military authority to give, and for that authority it was useless to apply to Fairfax, who, much as he sympathised with the soldiers in their grievances, had none of the revolutionary decision required by the situation. Cromwell, whose general approbation had probably been secured beforehand, now gave the required instructions, and Joyce was able to set out with the assurance that he was about to act under the orders of the Lieutenant-General.

There is reason to believe that Cromwell's instructions only gave authority for the removal of the King from Holmby conditionally on its appearing that he could in no other way be preserved from abduction by the Presbyterians. When on June 1 Joyce arrived at Oxford, he found that the garrison had resolved to refuse the delivery of the guns, and on the following day he marched on to Holmby with some 500 horsemen at his back. On his arrival Graves took to flight, and the garrison of the place at once fraternised with the new-comers. In the early morning of the 3rd Joyce, followed by his men, was let in by a back door asserting that he had come to hinder a plot 'to convey the King to London without directions of the Parliament'.

"His mission," he further stated, was "to prevent a second war discovered by the design of some men privately to take away the King, to the end he might side with that intended army to be raised; which, if effected, would be the utter undoing of the kingdom." To this profession his actions were suitable.

During the whole of the day he remained quiet, never hinting for an instant that he had any intention of doing more than preserve the King's person against violence. In the course of the day, however, he took alarm at some rumours of an impending attack, and made up his mind, probably nothing loth, that the danger could only be met by removing the King to safer quarters.

About half-past ten at night he roused Charles from his slumbers, invited him to follow him on the following morning, and on giving assurances that no harm would follow received the promise he required. On the morning of the 4th, as Charles stepped from the door of the house, he was confronted by Joyce and his 500 troopers. The King at once asked whether Joyce had any commission for what he was doing. "Here," replied Joyce, turning in the saddle as he spoke, and pointing to the soldiers he headed, "is my commission. It is behind me." "It is a fair commission," replied Charles, "and as well written as I have seen a commission in my life: a company of handsome, proper gentlemen, as I have seen a great while."

Having selected Newmarket as his place of residence, Charles not unwillingly, as it seemed, set out in this strange companionship. On that very morning, or on the previous evening, Cromwell, feeling himself no longer safe at Westminster, slipped away and rode off to join the army at Newmarket. Both Fairfax and

Cromwell declared for the King's return to Holmby, no doubt considering Joyce's removal of the King to be unnecessary, and, under the circumstances, unauthorised. It was only on Charles's positive refusal to return that he was allowed to continue his journey.

It would not be long before the army would have to experience the difficulties which beset a negotiation with Charles. It had first to come to an understanding with Parliament. Before Cromwell's arrival, the Agitators had presented to Fairfax a representation of their old complaints, accompanied with a reminder to Parliament that some particular persons—the Presbyterian leaders were evidently aimed at—had been to blame.

In another declaration, known as *A Solemn Engagement of the Army*, these complaints were more forcibly reiterated, with the addition, first of a demand for the erection of a Council of the army, composed partly of officers and partly of Agitators; and secondly, of a vindication of the army from harbouring wild schemes, 'such as to the overthrow of magistracy, the suppression or hindering of Presbytery, the establishment of Independent government, or the upholding of a general licentiousness in religion under pretence of liberty of conscience'. That these two clauses were added under Cromwell's influence—if not by his own pen—can hardly be doubted. On the one hand, if the army was to intervene in politics, it must speak through some organ, having, as far as possible, the character of a political assembly; and, on the other hand, it must be made clear to all that its aims were as little subversive as possible. If the Presbyterians would acknowledge that their designs had met with an insuperable obstacle, and would resign power into hands more likely to use it with prudence, the crisis might be tided over without leaving behind it more evil consequences than were necessarily connected with the intervention of an armed force.

Unhappily the Presbyterians were the most unlikely persons in the world to grasp the realities of the situation. They firmly believed, not only that their cause was just, but that the army—without a shadow of excuse—had deliberately, even before the London militia had been reorganised, plotted the seizure of the King's person, with the object of establishing anarchy in the Church and military despotism in the State.

Each party, in short, was convinced that it was acting on the defensive; and, in politics, as in all other spheres of life, results are to be traced less to facts which actually exist than to the assumptions relating to those facts in the minds of the actors. Parliament actively pursued its preparations for resistance, planning the formation of the nucleus of a fresh army at Worcester, and granting permission to the City to raise cavalry as well as infantry. The soldiers were undoubtedly right in holding that nothing less than the outbreak of another civil war was impending.

Before the irrevocable step was taken, Parliament sent commissioners to persuade the army to disband on the payment of an additional £10,000. On the 10th, the commissioners finding the soldiers at a rendezvous on Triploe Heath were received by a general refusal to accept the terms till they had been examined by the new Army Council. The army then significantly marched to Royston, several miles on the road to London.

In the evening a letter was sent off to the magistrates of the City, the chief supporters of the new Presbyterian military organisation. It can hardly be questioned that this letter represented the ideas at that time entertained by Cromwell, or that in great part, if not entirely, it was written by him. Striving to blind himself to the fact that he was heading military resistance to the civil power, he announced that those in whose name he spoke were acting, not as soldiers, but as Englishmen. "We desire," he proceeded, "a settlement of the kingdom and of the liberties of the subject according to the votes and declarations of Parliament which, before we took up arms, were by Parliament used as arguments and inducements to invite us and divers of our dear friends out—some of whom have lost their lives in this war, which being by God's blessing finished, we think we have as much right to demand and see a happy settlement, as we have to our money, or the other common interest of soldiers that we have insisted upon." Then followed a renewal of the protest that the army had no wish to introduce licentious liberty, or to subvert the Civil Government. "We profess," continued Cromwell, "as ever in these things, when the State has once made a settlement, we have nothing to say, but submit or suffer. Only we could wish that every good citizen and every man that walks peacefully in a blameless conversation, may have liberties and encouragements, it being according to the just policy of all States, even to justice itself." Then followed the practical conclusion. "These things are our desires—beyond which we shall not go, and for the obtaining these things we are drawing near your city—declaring with all confidence and assurance that, if you appear not against us in these our just desires, to assist that wicked party that would embroil us and the kingdom, neither we nor our soldiers shall give you the least offence." Should things proceed otherwise, it would not be the army that would give way. "If after all this," continued Cromwell, "you, or aconsiderable number of you, be seduced to take up arms in opposition to, or hindrance of these our just undertakings, we hope, by this brotherly premonition, we have freed ourselves from all that ruin which may befall that great and populous city; having hereby washed our hands thereof."

▲ The Edgehill monument stone

The army marched, and the City at once made its submission. The bare facts of the case told heavily against Cromwell in the eyes of those whose schemes he had frustrated. In May he had protested that the army would disband at a word from Parliament, and had renounced all thought of bringing military force to control affairs of State. In June he had made himself the leader of the army to disperse a force which was being raised by the orders of Parliament. The very words in which he, writing in the army's name, had announced his decision must also have told against him. It would have been far better if he had simply announced that the new circumstances which had arisen had forced upon him the conviction that he had gone too far and had driven him to acknowledge to himself and others that obedience to a Parliament might have its limits, and that those limits had now been reached. The line, it would have been easy to say, must be drawn when Parliament was preparing civil war, not in defence of the rights of Englishmen, but to impose upon the country a system alien to its habits with the assistance of a Scottish army. Unhappily it was in Cromwell's nature to meet the difficulty in another way. When most inconsistent he loved to persuade himself that he had always been consistent, and in taking refuge in the statement that the army put forward its claim to be heard as Englishmen rather than as soldiers, he committed himself to a doctrine so manifestly absurd that it could only be received with a smile of contemptuous disbelief. Cromwell, in fact, stood at the parting of the ways.

For him there was but one choice—the choice between entire submission to Parliamentary authority and the establishment of military control. No wonder that he instinctively shrunk from acknowledging, even to himself, the enormous importance of the step he was taking: still less wonder that he did not recognise in advance the unavoidable consequences of the choice—the temporary success which follows in the wake of superior force, and the ultimate downfall of the cause which owes its acceptance to such means.

The immediate results developed themselves without long delay. The army, doing its best to carry on the work of violence under legal forms, proceeded to charge eleven of the leading Presbyterian members with attempting to throw the kingdom into fresh war, as well as with other misdemeanours.

The accused persons retaliated by pressing forward their scheme for gaining the assistance of a Scottish army, and for bringing up English forces devoted to their cause against the army under Fairfax and Cromwell. Fairfax and Cromwell were too near the centre of affairs to be so easily baffled by specious words. On June 26 a menacing letter from the army made the eleven members feel that their position was untenable, and voluntarily—so at least they asserted—they withdrew from their seats in Parliament. Who could now doubt that—under the thinnest of veils—the army had taken the supreme control of the government into its hands?

▲ English musketeer 1644

THE NEW MODEL ARMY AND THE KING

In his desire to escape from the undoubted evils of military government, Cromwell had the best part of the army behind him. Nor did it, at the moment, appear very difficult to attain this object by coming to terms with the King, especially as the army leaders were prepared to make concessions to Charles's religious scruples. Claiming freedom for themselves in matters of conscience, they were ready to concede it in return, and, for the first time since he had ridden out of Oxford, Charles was allowed to receive the ministrations of his own chaplains, and to join in offering prayer and praise in the familiar language of the Prayer Book of the Church. It was a long step towards the settlement of that religious question which had created so impassable a gulf between the King and the Presbyterians.

The constitutional question remained to be discussed, and the burden of framing terms to bind the King fell upon Cromwell's son-in-law, Ireton, rather than upon Cromwell himself.

Cromwell indeed would never have consented to see Charles replaced in the old position, but he was unskilled in constitutional niceties, and he left such details to others. The main difficulty of the situation was not long in revealing itself. Charles, who had been removed to Windsor, talked as if the dispute between the Houses and the soldiers might be referred to his decision. "Sir," replied Ireton, "you have an intention to be the arbitrator between Parliament and us; and we mean to be it between your Majesty and Parliament."

It was not that there was any definite constitutional idea in Charles's mind. With him it was rather a matter of feeling than of reason that he could occupy no other place in the State than that which tradition confirmed by his own experience had assigned to the man who wore the crown. For him as for another as weak for all purposes of government, as richly endowed with the artistic temperament as himself, Not all the waters of the salt, salt sea Could wash the balm from an anointed King.

Under whatever forms, Parliamentary or constitutional, he and no other was to be the supreme arbiter, empowered to speak in due season the decisive word—always just, always in the right. What was passing before his eyes did but confirm him in his delusion. There had been a quarrel between army and Parliament. Where was it to end unless he sat in judgment to dispense equity to both? Against that will—call it firm or obstinate, as we please—so inaccessible to the teaching of facts, so clinging to the ideas which had inspired his life, the pleadings of Cromwell and Ireton would be vain.

Of this Cromwell had no suspicion. He had never had personal dealings with the King, and had little insight into his peculiar character. On July 4 he saw him at Caversham, where Charles had been established, in order that he might be near Reading, now the head-quarters of the army. He fell at once under the charm of Charles's gracious manner, and fancied that a few days would bring about an agreement.

In full accord with Fairfax, he hoped to establish the throne on a constitutional and Parliamentary basis. Neither Charles nor any of those who were under his influence could understand the sincerity of this purpose. The French Ambassador, Bellièvre, seems to have sounded Cromwell on the object of his ambition, and to have received the memorable reply: "No one rises so high as he who knows not whither he is going".

To Sir John Berkeley, an ardent Royalist, Cromwell explained that the army asked only 'to have leave to live as subjects ought to do, and to preserve their consciences,' thinking that no man could enjoy his estates unless the King had his rights. Probably Cromwell, in his conversation, had emphasised the points which the army was willing to concede, and had minimised those on which it expected Charles to yield. Charles, at all events, was so convinced that the officers were prepared, almost unconditionally, to restore him to his former power, that he gave it as a reason for distrusting them, that they had not asked him for personal favours in return. There can be no doubt that Cromwell refrained at this time from pressing the King hardly.

He was present at the meeting of Charles with his children, now permitted to visit him for the first time since the beginning of the civil war. Himself a devoted father, he was touched by the affecting scene.

The King, he told Berkeley, was the 'uprightest and most conscientious man of his three kingdoms'. Yet he was too keen-sighted to be blind to the other side of his character. He wished, he said, that his Majesty would be more frank and not so strictly tied to narrow maxims.

Already Cromwell's apparent devotion to the King's person was not unnaturally drawing forth harsh criticisms from those who failed to understand the essential unity underlying divergencies in his action.

Some at least amongst the Agitators were joining the Presbyterians in sarcasms directed against the man who was everything by turns; who had at one time taken the Covenant—at another time accepted the disbandment of the army; at another time again had made himself the instrument of the army in its resistance of disbandment. Cromwell took no notice of such calumnies. He was more concerned with the eagerness of the Agitators to march upon Westminster with the object of forcing the Houses to condemn the eleven members who were again stirring, and of crushing the discontent which was simmering amongst the City population.

Happily the mere threat of force had been sufficient, and Parliament virtually abandoned its hostile attitude by naming Fairfax Commander-in-chief of all the forces in the country. Would it be so easy to deal with Charles? By July 23, The Heads of the Proposals, probably drawn up by Ireton—who, of all the officers, was the most versed in constitutional lore—with the assistance of Colonel Lambert, having been adopted by the Army Council, were submitted to the King. So far as religion was concerned, they anticipated the settlement of the Revolution of 1688, leaving all forms of worship—including that of the condemned Prayer Book—to the voluntary choice of the worshipper. So far as politics were concerned, provision was to be made, not merely for making the King responsible to Parliament, but for making Parliament responsible to the people. There were to be biennial Parliaments, elected by enlarged constituencies, and a Council of State was to be formed, to whose consent in important matters the King was to bow.

The first Council was to remain in office for at least seven years. How it was to be nominated after that was left uncertain, probably till the question had been threshed out in discussion with the King.

The army leaders had yet to discover how little profit such a discussion would bring. Charles was not prepared to abandon his old position for that of constitutional King, limited, as he had never been limited before, by opposing forces. If he had spoken his objections clearly out it would have been easy to criticise him as one who was blind to the forces which were governing events: it would have been impossible to hold him morally at fault. The course which he took could not but lead to disaster.

Listening to the army leaders, he yet conspired against them, still placing his hopes on the assistance of a Scottish army, and speculating on the chances of a breach between the army on the one side and the Parliament and the City on the other, which would enable him to grasp the reins of power under the old conditions. “I shall see them glad ere long,” he told Berkeley, “to accept more equal terms.” He even went so far as to imagine that Fairfax and Cromwell were to be bribed by offers of personal advantage to re-establish his fallen throne on other terms than those now offered to him. “You cannot,” he told them, “do without me. You will fall into ruin if I do not sustain you.” He was partly supported by his knowledge that though the City authorities had yielded to the sway of the army, the City apprentices were in a state of disquiet and had broken into the House of Commons, compelling the members to vote a series of Presbyterian resolutions in defiance of the army. In misplaced confidence in this movement in the City, Charles entered into communication with Lauderdale, the ablest member of a body of Scottish Commissioners who had recently arrived nominally to urge the King to accept the Parliamentary terms, but in reality to negotiate a separate agreement between the Scots and the King. Charles eagerly closed with their proposals and allowed Lauderdale to send a message to Edinburgh urging the equipment of a Scottish army for the invasion of England. Unluckily for him, mob-violence was a feeble reed on which to lean.

The Speaker of the two Houses, together with the Independent members, took refuge with the army, and the army treating them as the genuine Parliament reconducted them to Westminster.

On August 6 Fairfax was named by the reconstituted Parliament Constable of the Tower, which though it had hitherto been guarded by the citizens was from henceforward to be garrisoned by a detachment of the army, whilst another detachment was left at Westminster as a guard to the Houses. The remainder of the soldiers, to show their power, tramped through the City, passing out by London Bridge on the march to Croydon—Cromwell riding at the head of the cavalry.

What could be the possible end of such demonstrations? Every time they were employed, the appeal to force was placed more clearly in evidence, in spite of all efforts to minimise it. Scarcely had the regiments filed out of the City when the Presbyterian majority reasserted itself in Parliament.

On the other hand, the Agitators raised their voices for a purge of Parliament which would thrust out those members who had sat and voted under the influence of the mob. Cromwell was growing impatient. “These men,” he said of the eleven members, some of whom had returned to their seats when the House was under the dominion of the mob, “will never leave till the army pull them out by the ears.” “I know nothing to the

contrary," he said on another occasion, speaking of Holles and Stapleton, "but that I am as well able to govern the kingdom as either of them."
On this, the eleven members left their seats for good and all, six of them taking refuge on the Continent.
Yet the majority in the Commons was Presbyterian still, and refused to vote at the dictation of the army. Cromwell's patience was exhausted.
On August 20 he brought a cavalry regiment into Hyde Park in order to obtain a vote that the proceedings of the House, in the absence of the Speaker, had been null and void. Under this threat, the majority gave way, and Cromwell, who had the whole army behind him, gained his immediate end. Once more he was drifting forwards in the direction of that military despotism which neither he nor his comrades desired to establish.
The one way of escape still lay in an understanding with the King.
With the King, however, no agreement was possible. Charles, hopelessly at fault in his judgment of passing events, stood aloof in the assurance that the strife amongst the opponents would serve but to weaken both.
In the negotiations carried on with the army simultaneously with the latest Parliamentary struggle, he fought every point stubbornly.
To extricate themselves from this difficulty, Cromwell and Ireton joined in a vote for resuscitating the Newcastle propositions, and allowed Charles to be formally requested to give his consent to those extravagant Presbyterian demands. Charles, driven to the wall, expressed his preference for The Heads of the Proposals. Cromwell and Ireton contrived to persuade themselves that he was in earnest, and gave their support to the King's demand for a personal negotiation with Parliament on that basis.

▲ English parliamentary pikemen sergeant

Under these circumstances the Independent party and the army split in two. The greater number of the superior officers, together with the Parliamentary leaders of the party, Vane, St. John and Fiennes, supported Cromwell and Ireton in an attempt to persuade Parliament to open the negotiations asked for by the King. As was not unnatural, there were others, Rainsborough in the army, and Marten in the House of Commons, who gathered round them a new Republican party, declaring it useless to enter into a fresh discussion with

Charles, and even talking of imprisoning him in some fortress. Coalescing with the Presbyterians, who wished merely to summon Charles to accept a selection from the Newcastle Propositions, they beat Cromwell on the vote, in spite of his warning that by disowning the King they were playing into the hands of men who 'were endeavouring to have no other power to rule but the sword'. Inside and outside the House Cromwell was denounced as a mere time-server, who had no other end in view but his own interests. Cromwell's only answer was to urge Charles more pressingly than before to make the concessions without which his restoration to any kind of authority was out of the question. Conscious of his own integrity, he still hoped for the best, even from Charles. "Though it may be for the present," he wrote to a friend, "a cloud may be over our actions to those who are not acquainted with the grounds of them, yet we doubt not God will clear our integrity and innocence from any other ends we aim at but His glory and the public good." Yet September passed away, and Charles had made no sign.

Charles's silence did but strengthen the party amongst the soldiers which aimed at cutting the political knot with the sword. In the Army Council indeed Cromwell was still predominant, and on October 6 it agreed to meet on the 14th, to formulate terms which the King might be able to accept. In the interval everything was done to come to a private understanding with Charles. Charles, however, was trusting to the probable Scottish invasion, and saw in the events taking place more closely under his eyes no more than a chance of discrediting Cromwell and his associates. When the Army Council met on the 14th, the subject of continuing the negotiations had to be dropped. The position was well explained in a letter from a Royalist. "The secret disposition," he wrote, "is that there is no manner of agreement between the King and the army; all this negotiation having produced no other effect but to incline some of the chief officers not to consent to his destruction, which I believe they will not, unless they be over-swayed; but cannot observe that they are so truly the King's as that they will pass the Rubicon for him, which if they could do, considering the inclination of the common soldiers, and generally of the people they might do what they would; but they are cold, and there is another faction of desperate fellows as hot as fire."

Almost, if not altogether, in despair, Cromwell sought a compromise with the Presbyterians on the basis of the temporary establishment of Presbyterianism as the national religion, with as large a toleration as he could persuade them to grant. When the House of Commons refused to extend toleration to the worship authorised by the Prayer Book, it was obvious that the scheme was not one which had a chance of obtaining the assent of Charles. Cromwell's hope of uniting Parliament and army in bringing pressure upon the King was as completely frustrated as his former hope of bringing about an understanding between the King and the army. His impotence could not but give encouragement to the other 'faction of desperate fellows as hot as fire' to demand a settlement on quite another basis from that on which Cromwell and the other army leaders had vainly attempted to found a Government.

In all his efforts, Cromwell's aim had been to strengthen the chances in favour of the new toleration by intertwining it with the old constitutional pillars of King and Parliament. His schemes, based as they were on a thoroughly political instinct which warned him against the danger of cutting the State adrift from its moorings, had broken down mainly in consequence of the resistance of the King.

It was but natural that earnest men should seek new modes of gaining their ends when the old ones proved ineffective. As the years of revolution passed swiftly on, new and more drastic schemes appeared upon the surface, not, as is often said, because in some unexplained way revolutions tend in themselves to strengthen the hands of extreme men, but because the force of conservative resistance calls forth moreviolent remedies. The misgovernment of Buckingham and Laud had fostered the Parliamentary idea. The resistance of Parliament to toleration had lcd to the conception by the army leaders of the idea of Parliamentary reform, and now the failure of those leaders produced the plan of founding a government not on institutions sanctified by old use and wont, but on a totally new democratic system. Outside the army, the main supporter of the new principles was John Lilburne, who had been a lieutenant-colonel in Manchester's army before the formation of the New Model, a man litigious and impracticable, but public-spirited and prepared to accept the consequences of his actions on behalf of his fellow-citizens or of himself. During the troubles he spent a great part of his life in prison, and at the present time he had been more than a year in the Tower.

He had a large following in thc army, and early in October five regiments deposed their Agitators, and choosing new ones, set them to draw up a political manifesto which, under the name of The Case of the Army

Truly Stated, was laid before Fairfax on the 18th.
The new thing in this scheme of the recently elected Agitators was not that they proposed to fix the institutions of the State by means of written terms. That had been done again and again by Parliament in various propositions submitted to Charles since the commencement of the Civil War, and more recently by the army leaders in The Heads of the Proposals. What was new was that they proposed in the first place to secure religious freedom and other rights by the erection of a paramount law unalterable by Parliament; and in the second place to establish a single House of Parliament—all mention of King or House of Lords was avoided—with full powers to call executive ministers to account—a House which was to be elected by manhood suffrage—an innovation which they justified on the ground that 'all power is originally and essentially in the whole body of the people of this nation'. It was a complete transition from the principles of the English Revolution to those of the French.
Against the foundation of a government on abstract principles, Cromwell's whole nature—consonant in this with that of the vast majority of the English people—rose in revolt. On the 20th he poured out his soul in the House of Commons in a three-hours' speech in praise of monarchy, urging the House to build up the shattered throne, disclaiming on behalf of the whole body of officers any part in the scheme of the party of the new Agitators, who were now beginning to be known as Levellers. It was to no purpose.
Monarchy without a King was itself but an abstract principle, and Charles would accept no conditions which would not leave him free to shake off any constitutional shackles imposed upon him. Only four days before the delivery of Cromwell's speech, Charles had assured the French Ambassador that he trusted in the divisions in the army, which would be sure to drive one or other of the disputants to his side.
The immediate result of Charles's resolution to play with the great questions at issue was an attempt by Cromwell and the officers to come to terms with the Levellers. On October 28 a meeting of the Army Council was held in Putney Church, to which several civilian Levellers were admitted, the most prominent of whom was Wildman, formerly a major in a now-disbanded regiment. Fairfax being out of health, Cromwell took the chair. The Agitators put the question in a common-sense form. "We sought," one of them said, "to satisfy all men, and it was well; but, in going to do it, we have dissatisfied all men.
We have laboured to please the King; and, I think, except we go about to cut all our throats, we shall not please him; and we have gone to support a House which will prove rotten studs. I mean the Parliament, which consists of a company of rotten members." Cromwell and Ireton—they continued—had attempted to settle the kingdom on the foundations of King and Parliament, but it was to be hoped that they would no longer persist in this course. Ireton could but answer that he would never join those who refused to 'attempt all ways that are possible to preserve both, and to make good use, and the best use that can be of both, for the kingdom'. The practical men had become dreamers, whilst the dreamers had become practical men. The Levellers, at least, had a definite proposal to make, whilst Cromwell and Ireton had none.
Since the appearance of The Case of the Army, the Agitators had reduced its chief requirements into a short constitution of four articles, which they called The Agreement of the People, intending, it would seem, to send it round the country for subscription, thus submitting it to what, in modern days, would be called a plebiscite, though apparently it was to be a plebiscite in which only affirmative votes were to be recorded. Nothing could be more logical than this attempt to find a basis of authority in the popular will, if the other basis of authority, the tradition of generations, was to be of necessity abandoned.
Cromwell, of all men in the world, was reduced to mere negative criticism. The proposal of the Agitators, he admitted, was plausible enough. "If," he said, "we could leap out of one condition into another that had so precious things in it as this hath, I suppose there would not be much dispute; though perhaps some of these things may be well disputed; and how do we know if, whilst we are disputing these things, another company of men shall gather together, and they shall put out a paper as plausible as this? I do not know why it may not be done by that time you have agreed upon this, or got hands to it, if that be the way; and not only another and another, but many of this kind; and if so, what do you think the consequence would be? Would it not be confusion?... But truly I think we are not only to consider what the consequences are ... but we are to consider the probability of the ways and means to accomplish it, that is to say that, according to reason and judgment, the spirits and temper of this nation are prepared to receive and go along with it, and that those great difficulties which lie in our way are in a likelihood to be either overcome or removed. Truly to anything

that's good, there's no doubt on it, objections may be made and framed, but let every honest man consider whether or no these be not very reasonable objections in point of difficulty; and I know a man may answer all difficulties with faith, and faith will answer all difficulties really where it is, as we are very apt all of us to call faith that perhaps may be but carnal imagination and carnal reasoning."

Not a word had Cromwell to say on behalf of any possible understanding with the King. All that he could do was to stave off a declaration in favour of the establishment of a democratic Republic, by proposing that the Army Council should reduce into formal shape the engagements entered upon at Newmarket and Triploe Heath. As those engagements had been put forward as demands to Parliament—not to the King, this suggestion at least thrust aside for the time being the thorny question of the possibility of coming to an understanding with Charles. Cromwell's proposal, however, was not likely to secure unanimity.

Wildman, on behalf of the Levellers, refused to be bound by engagements which he personally held to be unjust. On this Cromwell asked for the appointment of a committee to examine this question, as well as any others upon which there was a difference of opinion. He pleaded with his audience not to approach the matters in controversy 'as two contrary parties'. His hearers were in no temper to profit by the suggestion.

Wildman threw out a hint that if Parliament were to patch up an arrangement with the King, it would detract from natural right. The expression at once divided the assembly into two camps. Ireton declared that there was no such thing as natural right. Cromwell asked for the appointment of a committee to discuss the questions that had been raised about the engagements of the army. A Captain Audley sensibly urged the controversialists to remember that it was no time for empty disputation. "If we tarry long," he said, "the King will come and say who will be hanged first." Neither Audley's judicious remark, nor Cromwell's words thrown in from time to time in favour of peace, could stop the wrangle, which at least served to draw from Cromwell the nearest approach he ever made to the enunciation of a constitutional principle.

Though the Council of the Army, he declared, was not 'wedded and glued to forms of government,' it was prepared to maintain the doctrine that 'the foundation and the supremacy is in the people—radically in them—and to be set down by them in their representations,' in other words by their representatives in Parliament. To conciliate this doctrine with the upholding of the ancient constitution, reformed indeed, but unaltered in its main features, was the problem which the nation solved for itself in 1689, but which neither the nation nor Cromwell could contrive to solve so long as Charles I. refused to face the teaching of events.

On the following day, after a prayer-meeting held in compliance with a suggestion from the pious Colonel Goffe, the Army Council met again, to resolve, after long debate, to lay aside the consideration of the engagements of the army and to proceed at once to the examination of The Agreement of the People.

This determination was a check to Cromwell, who had proposed the committee. It was not long before his prudence was justified. A debate sprang up on the question of manhood suffrage, claimed by the Levellers as being in accordance with natural right, and rejected by their opponents, to whom natural right was a mere absurdity. After a fierce dispute, Cromwell did his best to persuade the meeting to avoid abstract considerations, and to content itself with the discussion of such questions as whether the existing franchise could be in any way improved. His characteristic tendency to look to the preservation of ancient rights finding no scope in any possible scheme for the retention of the monarchy, fixed itself on the question of the constitution of Parliament. Colonel Rainsborough, who, on questions relating to Parliamentary elections, was the chief speaker on the side of the Levellers, proposed an appeal from the Army Council to the Army at large. His proposal found no support and the Council broke up without coming to a decision.

After this Cromwell had his way. On the 30th the committee which he suggested, and on which both parties were represented, met to consider the points at issue. The constitutional scheme to which its assent was given followed the lines of The Heads of the Proposals more than those of The Agreement of the People.

It proposed reforms, not an entire shifting of the basis of government. Above all, it adhered to the view that the new constitution should come into existence by an agreement between King and Parliament—not by an appeal to the natural rights of man. In the long run Cromwell was justified by the event. On no other basis would the distressed nation find rest. His wisdom so far as present results were concerned was less conspicuous.

The next meeting of the Army Council was held under discouraging circumstances. Charles, who had for some time been established at Hampton Court, had refused to renew the parole which he had given, and it

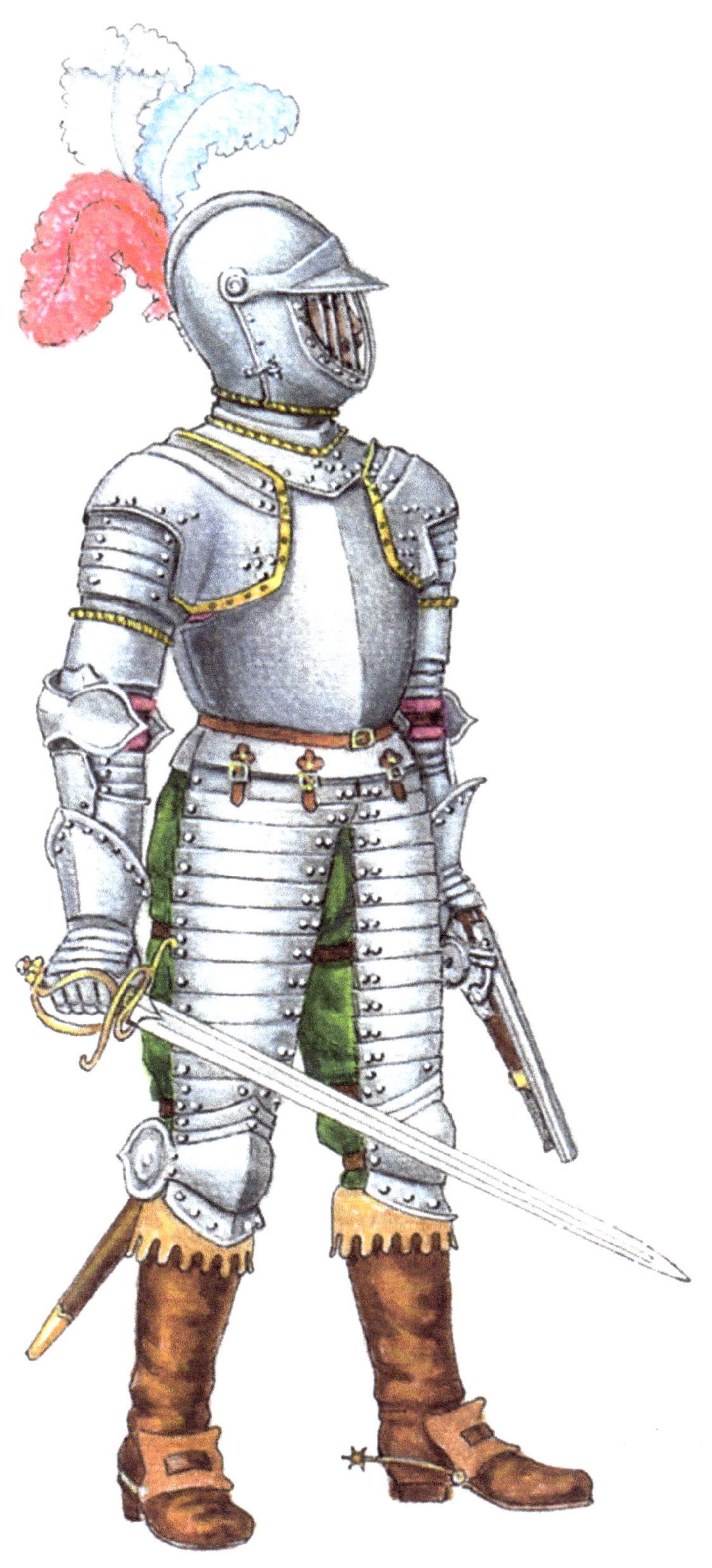

▲ English Heavy cavalry 1644

had been found necessary to strengthen his guards. Though there was no accurate knowledge at Putney of his intrigue with the Scots, enough had leaked out to raise grave suspicion, and when, on November 1, Cromwell again took the chair, he called on those present to 'speak their experiences as the issue of what God had given in answer to their prayers'. The result was distinctly unfavourable to the King.

One said that the negative voice of the King and Lords must be taken away; another that he could no longer pray for the King; a third that their liberties must be recovered by the sword. Cromwell did his best to stem the tide. Pointing out, just as a modern historian might do, that there had been faults on both sides, he called on 'him that was without sin amongst them to cast the first stone'. He then turned to the more practical question of the difficulty of maintaining discipline in the army, if the authority of Parliament were shut off. "If there be no Parliament," he argued, "they are nothing, and we are nothing likewise."

Though Cromwell was not yet prepared to strike at the King, he no longer regarded his comprehension in the new constitution as absolutely essential. He was even ready to accept the new democratic basis of The Agreement of the People, if there should be a wide demand for it.

He must look, he said, for 'a visible presence of the people, either by subscriptions or numbers—for in the government of nations that which is to be looked after is the affections of the people'. For the present, however, he seemed most inclined to trust in Parliament as the source of authority.

On one thing he was clear, that the discipline of the army must not be ruined by such an appeal to the general body of the soldiers in support of the Agreement as Rainsborough had contemplated. "I must confess," he said, "that I have a commission from the General, and I understand what I am to do by it.

I shall conform to him according to the rules and discipline of war ... and therefore I conceive it is not in the power of any particular men, or any particular man in the army, to call a rendezvous of a troop, or regiment, or in the least to disoblige the army from the commands of the General.... Therefore I shall move what we shall centre upon. If it have but the face of authority, if it be but a hare swimming over the Thames I will take hold of it rather than let it go."

It was hard, indeed, in those days, to say where the face of authority was to be found, and Cromwell was far from being able to solve the question. The most innocent suggestion made by his opponents was that the army must purge Parliament and declare the King responsible for the ruin of the country.

Goffe declared that it had been revealed to him that the sin of the army lay in its tampering with God's enemies, in other words, with Charles. Cromwell struck in with an expression of distrust in personal revelations. He himself, he explained, was guided by God's dispensations, that is to say, in more modern phrase, by the requirements of the situation. He acknowledged that danger was to be apprehended from the King and House of Lords, and that it was not his intention 'to preserve the one or the other with a visible danger and destruction to the people and the public interest'. On the other hand, he refused to accept it as certain that God had determined to destroy King and Lords, though he thought it probable that it was so. In the end, the constitutional discussion was transferred to a committee.

For a right judgment of Cromwell's character and habits of procedure no evidence exists of such importance as that which has been thus summarised. Here at least is laid bare before us his reluctance to abandon an untenable position, long after it has become clear to more impatient spirits that it has become untenable. Yet his hesitation is not based on any timorous reluctance to act.

It arises from his keen sense of the danger of any alternative policy, a sense which will be overmastered as soon as action in one direction or the other becomes a manifest necessity. On November 8, seeing that the Levellers were bent on pushing forward their proposal of manhood suffrage, he obtained a vote from the Army Council directing that both officers and Agitators should be sent back to their regiments.

There can be little doubt that the danger was greater than was thus indicated, and that there was truth in a story which charged the Levellers with intending, at this time, to purge the Parliament and to bring the King to trial. On the 11th, at all events, the brave but fanatical Colonel Harrison was calling for the prosecution of the King, and on the same day Cromwell sent to Whalley, who commanded the guard at Hampton Court, to provide against any attempt on Charles's person. Similar warnings had reached Charles himself, and on the evening of the same day he quietly made his escape.

On the 14th, after the failure of a scheme for the provision of a vessel from Southampton to carry him to France, he reached Carisbrooke, where the Governor of the Castle was Robert Hammond, Cromwell's cousin.

Cromwell's first task was to ensure the discipline of the army. His persistent efforts to keep up negotiation with the King had exposed him to the distrust of the Levellers, and it is said that some of them had resolved to murder him in his bed. There was no time to be lost.

On the 15th a rendezvous of a third part of the army was to be held on Corkbush Field, not far from Ware, and there could be no doubt that the Levellers would make desperate attempts to seduce the regiments from their military obedience. To meet the danger, a manifesto was issued in the name of Fairfax and the Army Council, in which Fairfax offered to give his support to the early dissolution of Parliament and to a plan for making the House of Commons 'as near as may be, an equal representative of the people that are to elect'.

For the rest, every soldier would be expected to sign a form of adhesion to the General and the Council. Speaking broadly, the conflict was between the men who knew the importance of maintaining the discipline of the army, and those who would reduce it to an armed mob eager to compel Parliament to adopt the democratic system of The Agreement of the People. On the 15th the soldiers gathered to the appointed rendezvous on Corkbush Field, where most of the regiments, with more or less reluctance, submitted to their officers. Two, those of Harrison and Robert Lilburne, both of which had been ordered elsewhere, mutinously made their appearance with copies of The Agreement of the People in their hats, as well as the motto "England's Freedom! Soldiers' Rights!" A few words from Fairfax reduced Harrison's regiment to obedience.

Cromwell, finding that Lilburne's men defied his order to remove the papers from their hats, rode into the ranks with his sword drawn, on which the regiment, with one accord, did as it was bidden. Three of the ringleaders were condemned to death by a court-martial held on the spot, and then ordered to throw dice for their lives. He who threw lowest was shot in the presence of the whole force, and the mutiny was brought to an end.

By this time the weary round of negotiation was beginning afresh. Charles sent up new proposals to the Parliament, proposals which, if he were in earnest, might possibly serve as a foundation for an agreement.

It concerned Parliament and army alike to discover whether Charles, who for many months had shown no sign of eagerness for settlement, was now aiming at anything more than an excuse to enable him to gain time for an arrangement with the Scots. So suspicious had the officers grown that Ireton was heard to say that if peace were to be made between King and Parliament, he hoped it would be such as that the army 'might, with a safe conscience, fight against both'.

If we are to believe a story, told indeed only after the Restoration, but which has inherent probability in it, Cromwell and Ireton, having reason to suppose that a letter from Charles to the Queen would be carried by a man who was to stay the night at the Blue Boar in Holborn, disguised themselves as troopers, and waited in the inn drinking beer till the messenger arrived. Then, ripping up his saddle, they found the expected letter, from which they learnt that 'the King had acquainted the Queen that he was now courted by both the factions, the Scotch Presbyterians and the army, and which bid fairest for him should have him, but he thought he should close with the Scots sooner than the other'. According to another account, the letter also assured Henrietta Maria that she need not concern herself about any concessions he might make, as 'he should not look upon himself as obliged to keep any promises made so much on compulsion whenever he had power enough to break them'.

Whatever may be the exact truth about the intercepted letter, it is exceedingly likely that Cromwell, in some way or other, received intelligence which confirmed his growing belief in Charles's untrustworthiness.

This view of the case is confirmed by the fact that, not long after, the Parliament prepared four Bills, not as a basis of a settlement, but as a test to show whether Charles was in earnest or not, principally by asking him to abandon his control over the militia. On the other hand Charles so misconceived his position as to send Berkeley to Fairfax with a request that he would support him in asking for a personal treaty unfettered by any conditions whatsoever. When, on November 28, Berkeley arrived at head-quarters, Fairfax briefly referred him to Parliament, whilst neither Cromwell nor Ireton would enter into conversation with him.

To the soldiers who had mistrusted him Cromwell professed 'that the glories of this world had so dazzled his eyes that he could not discern clearly the great works the Lord was doing; that he was resolved to humble himself, and desired the prayers of the saints, that God would be pleased to forgive his self-seeking'.

On the following morning he sent a message to Berkeley in a more worldly strain, bidding him 'be assured he would serve His Majesty as long as he could do it without his own ruin, but desired that he would not

▲ English Parliamentary cavalry 1644

expect that he should perish for his sake'. Such at least was the form given to the message by Berkeley when he wrote his Memoirs at a later date, and we may at least take it as established that Cromwell made it clear to Charles that, after what had happened, it was perfectly hopeless to expect the army to bring pressure on Parliament in his favour.

Charles turned to the Scots. There were two parties in Scotland—the party of the ministers of the Kirk, headed by the Marquis of Argyle, and the party of the nobility, headed by the Duke of Hamilton, of which the leading members were the Duke's brother, the Earl of Lanark, and the Earl of Lauderdale, both of whom, like many other Scottish nobles, had thrown themselves into the Presbyterian movement so long as it was directed against Bishops, but had rallied to the Crown as soon as the Ministers strove to make themselves independent of the nobility.

It was this latter party that was represented by the Scottish Commissioners in England, and on December 26 Charles signed an agreement with them—The Engagement, as it was called—which gave him his own way in England, allowing him to put an end to all toleration of the sects, and to grant a dominant position to Presbyterians for three years only. Against the English Parliament and the army the Scots were to claim for the Crown the power over the militia, the control over the Great Seal, the bestowal of honours and offices, the choice of Privy Councillors, and the negative voice in Parliament.

In support of this settlement, which included a disbandment of the army and a dissolution of Parliament, a Scottish army was to march into England. Of all the Scotsmen embarked in this scheme, the only man of marked ability was Lauderdale, and though no direct evidence exists on the subject, it seems likely enough that the Engagement was mainly, if not altogether, his work. If the suggestion be accepted that the picture by Janssen in the possession of the present Duke, in which a paper is being handed by Lauderdale to Lanark, represents the transference of the Engagement from the former to the latter, it would lend additional strength to the supposition founded on the relative intellectual powers of the two men.

However this may be, it is certain that two days after the signature of The Engagement, Charles rejected the Four Bills which had been laid before him by the English Parliament, thus showing his own belief that it was no longer needful for him to keep up even the semblance of an understanding with the Houses at Westminster.

That the result of a successful Scottish invasion would be to restore Charles to the throne on the old conditions, and to sweep away everything for which any English party had struggled, can hardly be doubted. It is true that The Engagement was buried in the garden of Carisbrooke Castle, and that not a word of its contents reached any English ears. Yet from the rejection of the Four Bills, following on the visit of the Scottish Commissioners to Carisbrooke, it was evident that some dangerous project was on foot, and even those who had welcomed a Scottish army in 1643, when it invaded England at their bidding, were likely to be scandalised at the intervention of another Scottish army in opposition to themselves.

To Cromwell and to the soldiers of every grade, the prospect of seeing those objects for which they had shed their blood wrenched from them by a Scottish invasion, was peculiarly offensive. In the army all quarrels were hushed and all offences pardoned in face of the obvious danger. What was more, the leading officers assured Parliament that the army might be relied upon against the invaders. The extreme Levellers indeed continued to regard Cromwell as a time-server and a hypocrite, and some even of those who were ready to accept his co-operation were somewhat suspicious. "If you prove not an honest man," said Hazlerigg to him, "I will never trust a fellow with a great nose for your sake."

Under the circumstances Charles's Royalist friends were sent away from Carisbrooke, and he himself, after a futile attempt to escape, treated as a prisoner under lock and key. A vote that no further addresses should be made to the King passed the Commons. For some time the Lords refused their concurrence, and it was only on a threat of the intervention of the army that they gave way. After the struggle was at an end, two regiments occupied Whitehall and the Mews. The supremacy of the army in the State was growing more pronounced as each political difficulty arose.

There are good reasons for believing that before the end of January, 1648, Cromwell, to whom the interference of the army in politics was almost as objectionable as the establishment of a democracy on abstract principles, proposed to transfer the Crown from Charles to the Prince of Wales; preserving the office whilst changing the persons. No proposal could have been more statesmanlike; but, unhappily, it was not possible to carry it into effect. The whole of the Royal family was too exasperated against the enemies of its head to lend itself to such a transaction. There can be no doubt that Cromwell had, by this time, abandoned all thought of looking to Charles as the basis of the political settlement he desired.

About the end of February a letter from Charles to the Queen was intercepted which convinced those into whose hands it fell that the writer was preparing to take the aggressive against his opponents.

Early in February Cromwell was found amongst the supporters of a Parliamentary declaration intended to uphold the vote of No Addresses, in which Charles's misdemeanours were set forth at length, somewhat in the fashion of the Grand Remonstrance. His attempt to bring into England Germans, Spaniards, Frenchmen, Lorrainers, and Danes as well as Irishmen was one of the principal counts against him. Cromwell is even said to have 'made a severe invective against monarchical government,' though it is probable that his argument was directed less against a hereditary chief-magistracy bound by constitutional limitations than against a system under which the King retained the ultimate decision of all questions in his own hands.

At all events, he refused to commit himself absolutely to Republicanism, thereby exasperating those who, like Marten, and even his own bosom friend—the younger Vane—had come to the conclusion that, in the England of that day, a Republic was the only alternative to an absolute monarchy.

It was about this time that a meeting took place, the proceedings at which were recorded by Edmund Ludlow, himself a Republican or Commonwealth's-man—to use the term in use amongst contemporaries.

Anxious to bring men of different opinions into line against Charles, Cromwell gave a dinner to the leaders of the various parties, after which a conference was held in which, according to Ludlow, Cromwell and his friends 'kept themselves in the clouds, and would not declare their judgments either for a monarchical, aristocratical or democratical government, maintaining that any of them might be good in themselves, or for us according as Providence should direct us'.

The old difference of opinion between the men of practice and the men of theory was, on this occasion, aggravated by the fact that many theoretical upholders of a Commonwealth drew the very practical conclusion that not only were Charles's subjects absolved from their allegiance, but that it was the duty of Parliament to call the King to account for the blood that had been shed in England in consequence of his misdeeds.

The conference begun in the interests of peace bade fair to lead to open division, and Cromwell, to silence angry vituperation, flung a cushion at Ludlow's head and ran downstairs. Ludlow in his turn threw the cushion back at Cromwell, and, as he proudly boasted, 'made him hasten down faster than he desired'.

A rough piece of horseplay, it at all events served its purpose in quieting a strife which, every minute that it lasted, was doing injury to the cause which Cromwell desired to serve.

At no time did Cromwell fix beforehand the methods by which he intended to work, though he never had any doubt of the object against which his energies were to be directed. He had contended first against irresponsible monarchical power, then in turn against military anarchy, Presbyterian tyranny, the political supremacy of the army, and abstract theories of government. He was ready to meet each danger as it arose, with the help of all who, whatever their opinions on other points might be, were ready to join him in attacking the abuse which he wished at the time to abate. If, like Ludlow, they persisted in looking too far ahead, there was nothing for it but to silence them, if it were but by flinging cushions at their heads.

In the Spring of 1648 Cromwell and his political allies had thus to deal with a very complicated situation. They had to face not merely Charles's intrigue with the Scots, but also the widely spread discontent in England. Especially in the towns, men were weary of military dictation, and of the increased taxation by which the army was supported. Parliament too was as unpopular as the army.

Englishmen were no less weary of the prolonged uncertainty which neither army nor Parliament seemed capable of bringing to an end. In their longing for a settled government, a considerable part of the population turned their eyes to the throne, as the ancient basis of authority and order.

If England had been polled, there would probably have been a large majority in favour of Charles's restoration to power, and yet, it was precisely amongst those whose system was most democratic that the most intense opposition to a restoration was to be found.

To Cromwell, man of order and discipline as he was, a restoration unaccompanied with security against the old mischief was intolerable. Of his own disinterestedness he gave at this time undeniable proof. Parliament having granted him lands valued at £1,680 a year, proceeded to reduce his pay at the same time that it reduced

▲ English pikeman 1644

▲ English musketeer 1644

that of other officers, by the large sum of £1,825. Far from taking umbrage at this diminution of his income, he presented not less than £5,000 to the public cause, and also abandoned the arrears due to him, which at that time amounted to £1,500. Certainly dangers were gathering thickly.

An intercepted letter from the King's agent at the Hague disclosed Charles's expectation to be succoured not only by an Irish army but by a Dutch one. Common prudence taught Cromwell to do everything in his power to conciliate any party that might stand by his side against so extensive a combination.

When his scheme for placing the Prince of Wales on the throne was revived about the middle of March, some of the Episcopal clergy preferred an understanding with the army to an understanding with the Scots. Towards the end of the month, Cromwell was still in negotiation with members of the Royalist party, the purport of which it is impossible to define, but which probably had its rise in his persistent desire to maintain royalty in some shape or form as a basis of order.

It is at least certain that he gained much obloquy from his own party. "I know," he wrote to a friend, "God has been above all ill reports, and will in His own time vindicate me. I have no cause to complain." It was never Cromwell's way to answer calumny by a public explanation of his conduct.

At last, however, Cromwell came to the conclusion that nothing was to be hoped from an understanding with the Royalists; and it therefore became more necessary to secure the co-operation of the English Presbyterians. An attempt to win the City Magistrates by concessions was, however, promptly repulsed.

On April 6 it became known in London that Charles had all but succeeded in effecting his escape, and on the 9th a City mob was rushing westwards along the Strand with the intention of overpowering the soldiers at Whitehall and the Mews. A charge of cavalry ordered by Cromwell drove them back, but it was not till the following day that the tumult was suppressed. All this while the Hamilton party, which was keen for an invasion of England, was gaining strength in Scotland.

So black did the outlook become that one more appeal was made to the King, and there are strong reasons for believing that he was warned that, if he persisted in refusing compliance to the demands made upon him—whatever they may have been—Parliament would proceed, on April 24, to depose him, and to crown the Duke of York, who was still in their hands, as James II.

Charles replied by sanctioning a plan for his son's escape, and before the appointed day arrived the boy was well on his way to the Continent.

The first resistance to Parliament came from an unexpected quarter. As early as on February 22, Colonel Poyer, the Governor of Pembroke Castle, had refused to deliver up his charge till his arrears had been paid, and on March 23 he had proceeded to seize the town. At first no more than a local difficulty was apprehended, and Colonel Horton was despatched to suppress the rising.

On his arrival he wrote that he was likely to have the whole of South Wales on his hands. Almost at the same time it was known at Westminster that a Scottish army was actually to be raised. Presbyterian as was the majority of the English Parliament, it had no mind to have even its favourite religion established by an invading army of Scots, especially as that army would be the army of the Scottish nobility, who were supposed not to feel any warm attachment to the Presbyterian cause except so far as their own interests were connected with it. It was the hesitation of the English Presbyterians between their political and their ecclesiastical aims which alone could have given a free hand to Fairfax and Cromwell. It was Cromwell who, seconded by Vane, carried a vote in the House for granting concessions which the City under the pressure of the recent intelligence, was now prepared to accept as satisfactory.

A further vote that the House would not alter the fundamental government of the kingdom by King, Lords and Commons, was supported by the leading Independents. The House then proceeded to declare itself ready to concur in a settlement on the ground of the propositions laid before the King at Hampton Court, that is to say, on the ground of the establishment of Presbyterianism without any liberty of conscience whatsoever. Whether Cromwell was in his place when the last two votes were taken is uncertain.

At all events we can hardly be wrong in supposing that he had no objection to the Presbyterians amusing themselves with another hopeless negotiation whilst the army took the field. He had had too much experience of Charles's character as a diplomatist to imagine that he was likely to aim at anything more than hoodwinking his opponents till the time came when he might deem it advisable to hoodwink his allies.

Cromwell's presence was imperatively needed at head-quarters, which were now established at Windsor.

▲ English musketeer 1645

He found the army in an agitated condition, and we may well believe that his own feelings were no less agitated. The peaceful settlement which he had so long pursued seemed farther off than ever, and he can have brought with him no friendly thoughts of a King who would neither accept reasonable terms for himself, nor abdicate in favour of those who would.
On April 29 the chief men of the army held a prayer-meeting to inquire 'into the causes of that sad dispensation,' and in a discussion which followed on the 30th Cromwell urged those present thoroughly to consider their actions as an army and their conduct as private Christians, that they might discover the cause of 'such sad rebukes' as were upon them by reason of their iniquities.
That day no definite result was arrived at, but on the next, news having arrived that the forces in Wales had suffered a check, Fairfax ordered Cromwell to take the command in those parts.
Before Cromwell set out for his new command one more meeting was held. "Presently," we are told by one who was present, "we were led and helped to a clear agreement amongst ourselves, not any dissenting, that it was the duty of our day, with the forces we had, to go out and fight against those potent enemies which that year in all places appeared against us, with humble confidence, in the name of the Lord only, that we should destroy them; also enabling us then, after serious seeking His face, to come to a very clear and joint resolution on many grounds at large then debated amongst us, that it was our duty, if ever the Lord brought us back again in peace, to call Charles Stuart, that man of blood, to an account for the blood he had shed and mischief he had done to his utmost against the Lord's cause and people in these poor nations."
To what other conclusion could these men possibly come? How were they likely to recognise the deeply seated belief in the justice of his Church and cause which lay behind the slippery trickiness of Charles? and how, even if they had recognised it, could they have counted it to him for righteousness?
For many a month Cromwell had staved off this decision. Now, he could not reconcile it to his conscience to stave it off any longer; his conscience in this, no doubt, concurring with his interests. He left the Presbyterians at Westminster to their own devices—to pass an ordinance which imposed the bitterest penalties on heresy, and to toy with the idea of a fresh negotiation with Charles, content that they had been brought into line with the army in opposition to a Cavalier insurrection at home and a Scottish invasion from abroad.
Every indication served to convince the Houses of the Royalist character of the insurrection.
There were tumults either actually breaking out or threatened in Suffolk, in Essex and in Surrey, and in every case a resolution to support the King was either declared or implied. Such a development was no more to the taste of the Presbyterians than to that of the soldiers, and the army was therefore able to calculate on the support of a Parliament which, though it might detest the principles of the soldiers, was unable to dispense with their services.
That army was not one to be easily defeated. Before Cromwell reached his appointed station, he heard that Horton had overcome the Welshmen at St. Fagans. The political effect of the victory was immense. "To observe the strange alteration," wrote a London Independent to a friend in the army, "the defeating of the Welsh hath made in all sorts is admirable. The disaffected to the army of the religious Presbyterians now fawn upon them—partly for fear of you, and partly in that they think you will keep down the Royal party which threatened them, in their doors, in the streets, to their faces with destruction, and put no difference between Presbyterian and Independent."
On May 19 the Common Council of the City declared its readiness to live and die with the Parliament, at the same time requesting that a fresh negotiation should be opened with the King—a proposal which was at once accepted. The Royalists were bitterly disappointed. "How long," jibed one of them, "halt ye between two opinions? If Mammon be God, serve him; if the Lord be God, serve Him. If Fairfax be King, serve him; if Charles be King, restore him." To Fairfax and Cromwell the decision of the City must have come as a great relief. The work before them was hard enough, but there was no longer reason to despair.
So far as Fairfax was concerned, it had been intended that he should march against the Scots whilst Cromwell marched into Wales. A rising in Kent, followed by the defection of part of the navy, frustrated this design.
On June 1 Fairfax defeated the Kentish Royalists at Maidstone, but a part of their forces crossing the Thames threw themselves into Essex in the hope of rallying the Royalists of the eastern counties to their side.
Fairfax after a magnificently rapid march penned them into Colchester, where they could only be reduced by a long and tedious blockade. At the same time Cromwell, having pushed on through South Wales, was

occupied with the siege of Pembroke Castle, which did not surrender till July 11, thus leaving full time for the completion of the Scottish preparations. "I pray God," he had written to Fairfax whilst as yet the issue was undecided, "teach this nation and those that are over us, and your Excellency and all us that are under you, what the mind of God may be in all this, and what our duty is.

Surely it is not that the poor godly people of this kingdom should still be made the object of wrath and anger, nor that our God would have our necks under a yoke of bondage; for these things that have lately come to pass have been the wonderful works of God breaking the rod of the oppressor as in the day of Midian, not with garments much rolled in blood, but by the terror of the Lord, who will yet save His people and confound His enemies."

What a light is thrown upon Cromwell's thoughts by these words! No Parliamentary supremacy or rule of the majority—not even a general toleration after the fashion of Roger Williams or Milton was uppermost in his mind. Security for those whom he styled 'the poor godly people' was the main object of his striving, though he was too large-minded not to assign an important, if but a secondary place, to questions relating to the fall or preservation of Kings and Parliaments, as the institutional framework of political order without which even 'the poor godly people' could not enter the haven of safety.

Three days before Cromwell was released from Pembroke the Scottish army under the Duke of Hamilton had crossed the Border, sending before it a declaration against toleration either for the Common Prayer Book or for the worship of the sects. It was unlikely that if Charles were restored by Hamilton's means he would be required to fulfil more than that portion of the declaration which related to the repression of the sects.

The Hamilton party, as the secular party in Scotland, was devoid of enthusiasm, and anxious to throw off the yoke of the clergy. Hamilton, however, was a most incompetent general. He and his army, in short, had no advantage but that of numbers over the well-disciplined and fiery enthusiasts who followed Cromwell.

They neither trusted God nor kept their powder dry.

Though the invading army entered England by way of Carlisle, Cromwell marched against them not through Lancashire but through Yorkshire. He had to supply his men with shoes and stockings from Northampton and Coventry, and to halt at Doncaster to pick up the artillery which was forwarded him from Hull, as well as to rejoin Lambert, who was in command of the small force which it had been possible to despatch to the North whilst Cromwell was detained at Pembroke, and who had been doing his best to delay the progress of the Scots till Cromwell was ready to strike home.

On its march through Lancashire, Hamilton's army, some 21,000 strong, pushed slowly forward in a long straggling column, the van and the rear at too great distance from each other to be able to concentrate in case of an attack. On August 17, when Cromwell had crossed the hills into Ribblesdale and was close at hand upon his left flank, Hamilton, who had pushed on his cavalry to Wigan sixteen miles in advance, sent the bulk of his infantry across the Ribble at Preston, leaving Sir Marmaduke Langdale with 3,600 English Royalists on the north bank, whilst another detachment was some miles in the rear.

It did not need much generalship to overwhelm an army under such leadership as this. Cromwell fell upon Langdale, who had posted his small force to the greatest advantage behind hedges, and after a hard tussle, carried the position and captured the greater part of the division. Then lining the steep northern bank of the Ribble with musketeers, he drove Hamilton from the flat southern bank and, later on, across the Darwen which, near this point, flows into the Ribble. What followed was little more than mere pursuit.

The Scots, half starved and discouraged, were beaten wherever they attempted to make a stand, and Hamilton at last surrendered at Uttoxeter, eight days after the battle.

It was Cromwell's first victory in an independent command, and if the Scottish leader had played into his hands, he had been wanting in no part of an efficient general to profit by his folly.

Once more, in the despatch in which he announced his success to the Speaker, he harped upon the old string, the duty of the Parliamentary Government to give protection to the 'people of God'. "Surely, Sir," he wrote, "this is nothing but the hand of God, and wherever anything in this world is exalted or exalts itself, God will put it down; for this is the day wherein He alone will be exalted.

It is not fit for me to give advice, nor to say a word what use you should make of this; more than to pray you and all that acknowledge God, that they would take courage to do the work of the Lord in fulfilling the end of your magistracy in seeking the peace and welfare of this land; that all that will live peaceably may have countenance from you, and they that are incapable and will not leave troubling the land may speedily be destroyed out of the land."

On August 27, ten days after the victory at Preston, Colchester capitulated, and as far as England was concerned, the second civil war was brought to an end, only a few fortresses in the North—incapable of prolonged resistance without succour from any army in the field—still holding out.

It remained to be considered what policy should be adopted towards the defeated Scots, and first of all towards the thousands of prisoners captured at Preston and in the pursuit which followed. Of these a division was made—those who had been pressed into the service being set at liberty under an engagement never again to bear arms against the Parliament of England.

Those who had voluntarily taken service under Hamilton were transported to Barbados or Virginia, not, as is commonly said, as slaves, but as servants subjected for a term of years to a master who, though he usually dealt with them far more harshly than with his negro slaves, was at least bound to set them at liberty at the end of the appointed time.

The decision in this matter rested with Parliament not with Cromwell. It was for Cromwell to follow up the relics of the Scottish army left behind to the north of Preston, and which, after the defeat of their comrades, had retreated to Scotland. Nor could it be doubted that the word of the victorious general would have great weight with Parliament in that settlement of the outstanding complaints against Scotland which was now impending.

It was fortunate that this was so, as Cromwell was just the man to turn to the best advantage the dispute between the Scottish parties now bursting into a flame.

The defeat of Hamilton left the way open to Argyle and that party of the more fanatical clergy whose followers in the strongly Presbyterian West were known as Whiggamores, an appellation from which the later appellation of Whig was derived. The West rose in arms, and the Whiggamore Raid—as it was called—swept from power those few partisans of Hamilton who were still at liberty, and placed Scotland once more in the hands of Argyle and the clergy.

On September 21, whilst the conflict was yet undecided, Cromwell entered Scotland, demanding the surrender of Berwick and Carlisle, still occupied by Scottish garrisons. Argyle, glad of English support to strengthen his nascent authority, gave a hearty consent; and, to display the overwhelming strength of the English army to the Scottish people, Lambert was sent forward in advance, Cromwell following with the bulk of the army and arriving in Edinburgh on October 4.

On the 7th Cromwell returned to England, leaving Argyle under the protection of Lambert at the head of two regiments of horse. In the meanwhile Cromwell had come to an understanding with Argyle that no Scotsman who had supported the Engagement with Charles should be allowed to retain office, a stipulation as much in accordance with Argyle's wishes as with his own. A fanatic might have objected that it was unfitting that a tolerationist should give his support to the most intolerant clergy in Protestant Europe.

As a statesman, Cromwell could but remember that unless England were to assume the direct control over the Government of Scotland, it must leave such matters to local decision, especially as there were few or no Independents in Scotland to be wronged by any action which the new Government at Edinburgh might take. Yet there was undoubtedly a danger for the future in the divergency of aim between the followers of Argyle in Scotland and those of Cromwell in England.

Cromwell transferred his forces into Yorkshire to hasten the surrender of Pontefract and Scarborough, which still held out. The political interest of the day had shifted to the South. Parliament, as soon as it was relieved from danger, had determined to reopen the negotiation with the King, and the conference—known as The Treaty of Newport—commenced in the Isle of Wight on September 18.

In the regiments under Cromwell's command, as well as in Fairfax's army, the disgust was intense, and Ireton now took the lead in calling for a purge of the House which would get rid of such members as supported this piece of misplaced diplomacy. To complete the dissatisfaction of the army, the demands of Parliament included the establishment of Presbyterianism without a shadow of toleration on either hand.

It is unnecessary here to follow up this negotiation in detail. The objection taken to Charles's counter-proposals was less that they were themselves unjust, than that it was impossible to hinder him from slipping out of his promise whenever he felt strong enough to do so. Of this objection Ireton was the mouthpiece in Fairfax's army, and on or about November 10, he laid before the Council of officers the draft of a Remonstrance of the Army. It touched on many constitutional proposals, but the clause of the greatest practical interest asked 'that the capital and grand author of all our troubles, the person of the King, may be speedily brought to justice for the treason, blood and mischief he is therein guilty of'. The suggestion was too much for Fairfax, and he carried his officers with him in favour of a proposal that the army should ask the King to assent to the heads of a constitutional plan which would have reduced the functions of the Crown to that influence which is so beneficially exercised at the present day.

This proposal made to the King on the 16th was, however, rejected at once. The feeling of the army being what it was, Charles virtually signed his own death-warrant by this action, and it might seem to a superficial observer, as if his sufferings were due to his refusal to anticipate two centuries of history, and to abandon all the claims which had been handed down to him by his predecessors.

To the careful inquirer, it is evident that the causes of the army's demand lay far deeper. The men who made it were no constitutional pedants. It was the deep distrust with which Charles had inspired them that led to this drastic mode of setting him aside from the exercise of that authority which he had so constantly abused. It was his avoidance of open and honourable speech which brought Charles to the block.

Those who imagine that he was brought to the scaffold because of his refusal to submit to the abolition of episcopacy, forget that it had been in his power to secure the retention of episcopacy when it was offered him in The Heads of the Proposals, if only he had consented to its being accompanied by a complete toleration.

The effect of the news which Cromwell from time to time received from the army in England may be traced in the letters written by him at this time.

In one which he sent to Hammond on November 6 he justified his dealings with Argyle, suggesting that the example of Scotland, where one Parliament had been dissolved and another had been elected, might be followed in England.

In a second letter, written on the 20th, after he had had time to consider the rejection by Charles of the proposal of the army, he replied bitterly to an order of the House to send up Sir John Owen, a prisoner taken in Wales, that he might be banished. Cromwell angrily wrote that those who brought in the Scots had been adjudged traitors by Parliament, 'this being a more prodigious treason than any that had been perfected before; because the former quarrel was that Englishmen might rule over one another, this to vassalise us to a foreign nation, and their fault who have appeared in this summer's business is certainly double theirs who were in the first, because it is the repetition of the same offence against all the witnesses that God has borne, by making and abetting a second war'. "To vassalise us to a foreign nation." Here, in political matters at least, was the head and front of Charles's offending. It was this that finally broke down Cromwell's reluctance to shake himself loose from constituted authority. "God," Hammond had written, "hath appointed authorities among the nations, to which active or passive obedience is to be yielded. This resides in England in the Parliament. Therefore active or passive resistance is forbidden."

To this reasoning Cromwell replied, on the 25th, by various arguments, closing with the daring suggestion that the army might, after all, be 'a lawful power called by God to oppose and fight against the King upon some stated grounds; and, being in power to such ends,' might not they oppose 'one name of authority for these ends as well as another name'? Whatever might be the worth of these considerations, no good was to be expected from Charles. "Good," he protested, "by this man against whom the Lord hath witnessed, and whom thou knowest!"

Surely we have here laid bare before us Cromwellian opinion in the making. As in other men, the wish was father to the thought. The desire, whether for private or for public ends, shapes the thoughts, and in Cromwell's case, as the desires swept a wider compass than with most men, the thoughts took a larger scope and, to some extent, jostled with one another. The cloudy mixture would clear itself soon enough.

Meanwhile events followed quickly on one another in the south. Hammond, as too soft-hearted, was removed from Carisbrooke, and on December 1 emissaries from the army removed Charles to Hurst Castle, where he could be more easily isolated.

The foremost men in the army talked openly of putting the King to death, and adopted Cromwell's suggestion that Parliament should be forcibly dissolved, and a new one elected in its place. In this sense a Declaration was issued on November 30, and on December 2 the army marched into London. The Commons showed themselves to be unaffected by threats of violence, and voted on the 5th that the King's offers were 'a ground for the House to proceed upon for the settlement of the peace of the kingdom'.

The scheme of a dissolution favoured by the army was wrecked on the resistance of the Independent members of the House. There was to be a purge, not a dissolution followed by a general election. The plan thus agreed on was carried into practice on the morning of the 6th, when Colonel Pride stood with a military guard at the door of the House, turning back or arresting the members who had voted for a continuance of the negotiation with the King. When Cromwell returned to Westminster, on the evening of the same day, he declared that he had not 'been acquainted with the design; yet, since it was done, he was glad of it, and would endeavour to maintain it'.

As 'Pride's purge' had not been resolved on before the previous night it was physically impossible that he should have been informed of the resolution taken. There can be little doubt that he had given his sanction to the other plan of a dissolution, and had also concurred in the language ascribed to Ireton and Harrison on the previous evening. "Where," they had said of the House, "have we either law, warrant, or commission to purge it, or can anything justify us in doing it but the height of necessity to save the kingdom from a new war that they, with the conjunction of the King, will presently vote and declare for, and to procure a new and free representative, and so successive and free representatives, which this present Parliament will never suffer, and without which the freedoms of the nation are lost and gone!"

It will be worth while to remember these words, when the continuance of the now truncated Parliament was at last brought to an end.

It was Cromwell's habit to accept the second best, when the best proved unattainable. As to subjecting the King to a traitor's death, Cromwell, as on so many other occasions, exercised a moderating influence. Ireton, it seems, would have been satisfied if Charles were tried and sentenced, after which he might be left in prison till he consented 'to abandon his negative voice, to part from Church lands' and 'to abjure the Scots'.

Cromwell even wanted the trial itself to be deferred. By a small majority the Army Council resolved that Charles's life should be spared. As a last effort in this direction, Lord Denbigh was despatched to Windsor—to which place Charles had been removed—to lay before him conditions on which he might yet be permitted to live. Charles, who cannot but have known the nature of the overtures now brought, refused even to see the messenger.

Though no direct evidence has reached us, it can hardly be doubted that the terms offered included the renunciation of the negative voice and the abandonment of the Church, that is to say, of Bishops' lands; in other words, the abandonment of control over legislation and of episcopacy.

Here at last Charles found no possibility of evasion, and driven as he was to the wall, the true gold which was in him overlaid by so much ignorance and wrong-headedness revealed itself in all its purity. For him the only question was whether he should betray the ordinance of God in Church and State. The incapable ruler—the shifty intriguer—was at once revealed as the sufferer for conscience' sake.

Neither Cromwell nor his brother-officers had an inkling of this. To them Charles, in refusing this final overture, had asserted his right to be the persecutor of the godly and the obstructor of all beneficent legislation. Their patience was at length exhausted.

On January 1, 1649, an ordinance was sent up to the Lords creating a High Court of Justice for the trial of the King, accompanied by a resolution that 'by the fundamental laws of this kingdom it is treason in the King of England for the time being to levy war against the Parliament and Kingdom of England'. '

If any man whatsoever,' said Cromwell when this ordinance was under debate, 'hath carried on the design of deposing the King, and disinheriting his posterity; or, if any man hath yet such a design, he should be the greatest traitor and rebel in the world; but since the Providence of God hath cast this upon us, I cannot but submit to Providence, though I am not yet provided to give you advice'.

In the last words were the last symptoms of hesitation on Cromwell's part. Somehow or other all his efforts to save Charles from destruction had failed, and it was as much in Cromwell's nature to attribute the failure to Providence as it was in Charles's nature to regard himself as the earthly champion of the laws of God.

The House of Lords having refused to pass the ordinance, the House of Commons declared 'the people to be, under God, the original of all just power,' and in consequence, 'the Commons of England in Parliament assembled' to be capable of giving the force of law to their enactments. From this time forth the name of an Act was given to the laws passed by a single House. On January 6, such an Act erected a High Court of Justice for the trial of the King, on the ground that he had had a wicked design to subvert his people's rights, and with this object had levied war against them, and also, having been spared, had continued to raise new commotions.

Therefore, that no chief officer or magistrate might hereafter presume to contrive the enslaving or destroying of the nation, certain persons were appointed by whom Charles Stuart was to be tried.

Having once given his consent to the trial, Cromwell threw himself into the support of the resolution with all his vigour. "I tell you," he replied to some scruples of young Algernon Sidney on the score of legality, "we will cut off his head with the crown upon it." When a majority of the members of the Court refused to sit; when divisions of opinion arose amongst those who did sit; when difficulties, in short, of any kind arose, it was Cromwell who was ready with exhortation and persuasion to complete the work which they had taken in hand.

His arguments appear to have been directed not to the technical point whether Charles had levied war against the nation or not, but to convince all who would listen that there had been a breach of trust in his refusal to do his utmost for the preservation of the people. Charles, on the other hand, maintained, as he was well entitled to do, that he was not being tried by any known law, and that the violence used against him would lead to the establishment of a military despotism over the land.

Nothing he could say availed to change the determination of the grim masters of the hour. On January 27 sentence of death was pronounced by Bradshaw, the President of the Court, and on the 30th this sentence was carried into execution on a scaffold erected in front of the Banqueting House of his own palace of Whitehall. That Cromwell, once his mind made up, had contributed more than any other to this result can hardly be doubted. If we are to accept a traditional story which has much to recommend it, we have something of a key to his state of mind. "The night after King Charles was beheaded," we are told, "my Lord Southhampton and a friend of his got leave to sit up by the body in the Banqueting House at Whitehall.

As they were sitting very melancholy there, about two o'clock in the morning, they heard the tread of somebody coming very slowly upstairs. By-and-by the door opened, and a man entered very much muffled up in his cloak, and his face quite hid in it. He approached the body, considered it very attentively for some time, and then shook his head—sighed out the words, 'Cruel necessity!' He then departed in the same slow and concealed manner as he had come. Lord Southhampton used to say that he could not distinguish anything of his face, but that by his voice and gait he took him to be Oliver Cromwell."

Whether there was indeed any such necessity may be disputed for ever, as well as that other question whether the army had a right to force on the trial and execution in the teeth of the positive law of the land.

The main issue was whether, whatever positive law might say, a king was not bound by the necessities of his position to be the representative of the nation, acting on its behalf, merging his own interests in those of his people, refusing to coerce them by foreign armies, and owing to them, whenever it became prudent to speak at all, the duty of uttering words of simple truth. So Elizabeth had acted: so Bacon had taught. That Charles's own conduct was moulded on far different principles it is impossible to deny.

Confidence in his own wisdom was inherent in his nature, and there is no reason to doubt that he soberly believed his critics and antagonists to be so heated by faction that he was actually unable to do his best for the nation as well as for himself unless he called foreign armies to his aid, and raised false expectations in the hope of throwing off each party with whom he was treating, as soon as a convenient opportunity arrived. Such an attitude could not but engender resistance, and when long persisted in, necessarily called forth an attitude equally unbending.

That which to Cromwell was at one time a cruel necessity—at another time a decree of Providence—was but the natural result of the offence given by Charles to men who required plain dealing in a ruler from whom nothing but ill-concealed deceitfulness was to be had.

The final struggle had come to be mainly one over the King's retention of the Negative Voice, which, if he had been permitted to retain it, would enable him to hinder all new legislation which did not conform to his personal wishes.

No doubt he had both law and tradition on his side, but, on the other hand, his antagonists could plead that the law of the land must depend on the resolution, not of a single person, but of the nation itself.

“Fortunately or unfortunately,” I can but repeat here what I have already said elsewhere, “such abstract considerations seldom admit of direct application to politics.

It is at all times hard to discover what the wishes of a nation really are, and least of all can this be done amidst the fears and passions of a revolutionary struggle. Only after long years does a nation make clear its definite resolves, and, for this reason, wise statesmen—whether monarchical or republican—watch the currents of opinion, and submit to compromises which will enable the national sentiment to make its way without a succession of violent shocks. Charles's fault lay not so much in his claim to retain the Negative Voice, as in his absolute disregard of the conditions of the time, and of the feelings and opinions of every class of his subjects with which he happened to disagree.

Even if those who opposed Charles in the later stages of his career failed to rally the majority of the people to their side, they were undoubtedly acting in accordance with a permanent national demand for that government by compromise which slowly, but irresistibly, developed itself in the course of the century.

“Nor can it be doubted that, if Charles had, under any conditions, been permitted to reseat himself on the throne, he would quickly have provoked a new resistance. As long as he remained a factor in English politics, government by compromise was impossible.

His own conception of government was that of a wise prince, constantly interfering to check the madness of the people. In the Isle of Wight he wrote down with approval the lines in which Claudian, the servile poet of the Court of Honorius, declared it to be an error to give the name of slavery to the service of the best of princes, and asserted that liberty never had a greater charm than under a pious king.

Even on the scaffold he reminded his subjects that a share in government was nothing appertaining to the people. It was the tragedy of Charles's life that he was utterly unable to satisfy the cravings of those who inarticulately hoped for the establishment of a monarchy which, while it kept up the old traditions of the country, and thus saved England from a blind plunge into an unknown future, would yet allow the people of the country to be to some extent masters of their own destiny.

“Yet if Charles persistently alienated this large and important section of his subjects, so also did his most determined opponents. The very merits of the Independents—their love of toleration and of legal and political reform, together with their advocacy of democratic change—raised opposition in a nation which was prepared for none of these things, and drove them step by step to rely on armed strength rather than upon the free play of constitutional action. But for this, it is probable that the Vote of No Addresses would have received a practically unanimous support in the Parliament and the nation, and that in the beginning of 1648 Charles would have been dethroned, and a new government of some kind or other established with some hope of success.

As it was, in their despair of constitutional support, theIndependents were led, in spite of their better feelings, to the employment of the army as an instrument of government.

“The situation, complicated enough already, had been still further complicated by Charles's duplicity. Men who would have been willing to come to terms with him despaired of any constitutional arrangement in which he was to be a factor, and men who had been long alienated from him were irritated into active hostility.

By these he was regarded with increasing intensity as the one disturbing force with which no understanding was possible and no settled order consistent. To remove him out of the way appeared, even to those who had no thought of punishing him for past offences, to be the only possible road to peace for the troubled nation

It seemed that, so long as Charles lived, deluded nations and deluded parties would be stirred up by promises never intended to be fulfilled, to fling themselves, as they had flung themselves in the Second Civil War, against the new order of things which was struggling to establish itself in England.

“Of this latter class Cromwell made himself the mouthpiece. Himself a man of compromises, he had been thrust, sorely against his will, into direct antagonism with the uncompromising King. He had striven long to mediate between the old order and the new, first by restoring Charles as a constitutional King, and afterwards by substituting one of his children for him.

Failing in this, and angered by the persistence with which Charles stirred up Scottish armies and Irish armies against England, Cromwell finally associated himself with those who cried out most loudly for the King's blood. No one knew better than Cromwell that it was folly to cover the execution of the King with the semblance of constitutional propriety, and he may well have thought that, though law and constitution had both broken down, the first step to be taken towards their reconstruction was the infliction of the penalty of death upon the man who had shown himself so wanting in the elementary quality of veracity upon which laws and constitutions are built up. All that is known of Cromwell's conduct at the trial points to his contempt for the legal forms with which others were attempting to cover an action essentially illegal."

A further question which has been often mooted is whether Cromwell—whatever may be said on the purity of his motives—did not commit a blunder in respect of the interests of himself and his cause.

If those who have discussed this problem mean that the attempt to establish a free government during Cromwell's lifetime was rendered more difficult by the execution of the King, it is hard to gainsay their opinion, though the estrangement of the bulk of the population from the new order, in consequence of the execution, is probably very much exaggerated. Those who, like the Cavaliers, had been mulcted of a portion of their estates had an additional reason for detesting a government which had used them so ill, and there must have been a certain number amongst the crowds who read the Eikon Basilike—the little book in which Charles's vindication of his life was supposed to have been written by his own hand—who were permanently affected by that sentimental production of Dr. Gauden.

If, however, it is argued that Cromwell and his allies might possibly have succeeded in establishing a government to their taste if they had abstained from inflicting the last penalty on the King, it can only be answered that other causes made their success in the highest degree improbable.

Their plans for the benefit of the people were on the one hand too far advanced to secure popular support; and, on the other hand, too defective in fair-play to their opponents to deserve it. Puritanism was not, and never could be the national religion, and though it made more enemies through its virtues than through its defects, those who strove to enforce its moral and social precepts needed a strong military force at their backs.

The irritation caused by the interference of the army in religion and politics, and by the demands on the tax-payer which the maintenance of the army rendered necessary, would surely have been fatal to any government resting on such a basis, even if Charles had been suffered to prolong his days. If there remains any interest in Cromwell's career after the execution of the King it arises from his constantly renewed efforts to throw off this incubus, and his repeated failures to achieve his purpose.

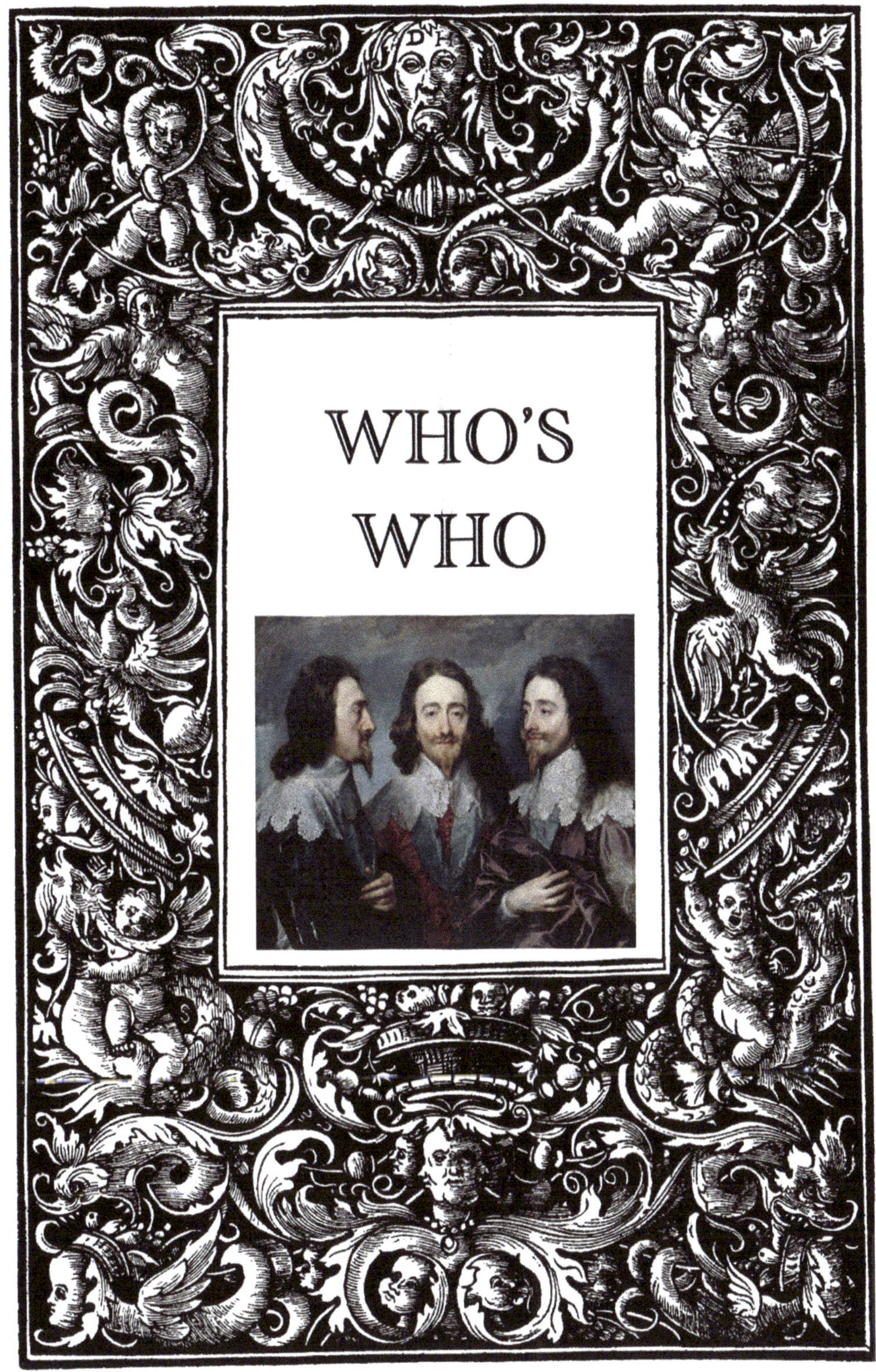
WHO'S
WHO

▲The Stuart royal family: Charles I and Henrietta Maria with his childrens and dogs.

WHO'S WHO

WHO IS CHARLES I KING OF ENGLAND, SCOTLAND AND IRELAND

Charles I (19 November 1600 – 30 January 1649) was monarch of the three kingdoms of England, Scotland, and Ireland from 27 March 1625 until his execution in 1649. Charles was the second son of King James VI of Scotland, but after his father inherited the English throne in 1603, he moved to England, where he spent much of the rest of his life. He became heir apparent to the English, Irish and Scottish thrones on the death of his elder brother in 1612. An unsuccessful and unpopular attempt to marry him to a Spanish Habsburg princess culminated in an eight-month visit to Spain in 1623 that demonstrated the futility of the marriage negotiations.

Two years later he married the Bourbon princess Henrietta Maria of France instead. After his succession, Charles quarrelled with the Parliament of England, which sought to curb his royal prerogative.

Charles believed in the divine right of kings and thought he could govern according to his own conscience. Many of his subjects opposed his policies, in particular the levying of taxes without parliamentary consent, and perceived his actions as those of a tyrannical absolute monarch. His religious policies, coupled with his marriage to a Roman Catholic, generated the antipathy and mistrust of reformed groups such as the Puritans and Calvinists, who thought his views too Catholic.

He supported high church ecclesiastics, such as Richard Montagu and William Laud, and failed to successfully aid Protestant forces during the Thirty Years' War. His attempts to force the Church of Scotland to adopt high Anglican practices led to the Bishops' Wars, strengthened the position of the English and Scottish parliaments and helped precipitate his own downfall.

The English Civil War

From 1642, Charles fought the armies of the English and Scottish parliaments in the English Civil War. After his defeat in 1645, he surrendered to a Scottish force that eventually handed him over to the English Parliament. Charles refused to accept his captors' demands for a constitutional monarchy, and temporarily escaped captivity in November 1647. Re-imprisoned on the Isle of Wight, Charles forged an alliance with Scotland, but by the end of 1648 Oliver Cromwell's New Model Army had consolidated its control over England. Charles was tried, convicted, and executed for high treason in January 1649. The monarchy was abolished and a republic called the Commonwealth of England was declared. In 1660, the English Interregnum ended when the monarchy was restored to Charles's son, Charles II.

WHO IS PRINCE RUPERT

Rupert, Count Palatine of the Rhine, Duke of Bavaria, 1st Duke of Cumberland, 1st Earl of Holderness, commonly called Prince Rupert of the Rhine, (17 December 1619 – 29 November 1682), was a noted German soldier, admiral, scientist, sportsman, colonial governor and amateur artist during the 17th century. Rupert was a younger son of the German prince Frederick V, Elector Palatine and his wife Elizabeth, the eldest daughter of James I of England. Thus Rupert was the nephew of King Charles I of England, who made him Duke of Cumberland and Earl of Holderness, and the first cousin of King Charles II of England.

His sister Electress Sophia was the mother of George I of Great Britain. Prince Rupert had a varied career. He was a soldier from a young age, fighting against Spain in the Netherlands during the Eighty Years' War (1568–1648), and against the Holy Roman Emperor in Germany during the Thirty Years' War (1618–48). Aged 23, he was appointed commander of the Royalist cavalry during the English Civil War (1642–46), becoming the archetypal Cavalier of the war and ultimately the senior Royalist general.

He surrendered after the fall of Bristol and was banished from England. He served under Louis XIV of France against Spain, and then as a Royalist privateer in the Caribbean. Following the Restoration, Rupert returned to England, becoming a senior British naval commander during the Second and Third Anglo-Dutch wars, engaging in scientific invention, art, and serving as the first Governor of the Hudson's Bay Company. Rupert died in England in 1682, aged 62.

▲ A young Prince Rupert, Count Palatinate, by Gerrit van Honthorst, circa 1641-1642

Prince Rupert is considered to have been a quick-thinking and energetic cavalry general, but ultimately undermined by his youthful impatience in dealing with his peers during the Civil War. In the Interregnum, Rupert continued the conflict against Parliament by sea from the Mediterranean to the Caribbean, showing considerable persistence in the face of adversity.

As the head of the Royal Navy in his later years, he showed greater maturity and made impressive and long-lasting contributions to the Royal Navy's doctrine and development.

As a colonial governor, Rupert shaped the political geography of modern Canada—Rupert's Land was named in his honour—and he played a role in the early African slave trade.

Rupert's varied and numerous scientific and administrative interests combined with his considerable artistic skills made him one of the more colourful individuals of the Restoration period.

WHO IS ROBERT DEVEREUX, 3RD EARL OF ESSEX

Robert Devereux, 3rd Earl of Essex KB PC (11 January 1591 – 14 September 1646) was an English Parliamentarian and soldier during the first half of the seventeenth century. With the start of the English Civil War in 1642 he became the first Captain-General and Chief Commander of the Parliamentarian army, also known as the Roundheads. However, he was unable and unwilling to score a decisive blow against the Royalist army of King Charles I.

He was eventually overshadowed by the ascendancy of Oliver Cromwell and Thomas Fairfax and resigned his commission in 1646. at the Battle of Edgehill Essex was the Parliamentarian commander of the army.

Essex's life guard included Henry Ireton, Charles Fleetwood, Thomas Harrison, Nathaniel Rich, Edmund Ludlow, Matthew Tomlinson and Francis Russell, all of whom played a leading role in the civil war and its aftermath. But a degree of amateurism and bad discipline was evident on both sides during the battle.

▲ Robert Devereux, 3rd Earl of Essex by Wenceslas Hollar 1642 about.

BIBLIOGRAPHY

-Battlefields Trust staff; Fletcher, Craig; Jones, Christopher (2013), Battle of Edgehill 23rd October 1642, The UK Battlefields Resource Centre, Battlefields Trust, retrieved 21 January 2013

-Carlton, Charles (1992), Going to the Wars: The Experience of the British Civil Wars, 1638-1651, Routledge, p. 192.

-Foard, Glenn (2009), Meller, H., ed., "The investigation of early modern battlefields in England", Schlachtfeldarchäeologie: Battlefield Archaeology, Halle, Germany: Lamdesmuseums für Vorgeschichte.

-Foard, Glenn; Morris, Richard (2012), The Archaeology of English Battlefields - Conflict in the Pre-Industrial Landscape, Council for British Archaeology, p. 121, ISBN 978-1-902771-88-5

-Miller, George (1896), Rambles round Edge Hills and in the Vale of the Red Horse [sic] (1st ed.), Banbury: William Potts.

-Evans, Martin Marix (2003), The Military Heritage of Britain and Ireland (2nd ed.).

-Steve Murdoch and Alexia Grosjean, Alexander Leslie and the Scottish Generals of the Thirty Years' War, 1618-1648 (Pickering & Chatto, London, 2014), pp. 120–123

-Roberts, Keith; Tincey, John (2001), Edgehill 1642: First Battle of the English Civil War, Osprey.

-The Scotsman staff (26 May 2006), "The final days of the old Scottish Regiments: 1709 Age no object in battle", The Scotsman

-Young, Peter (1995) [First published 1967], Edgehill 1642, Moreton-in-Marsh: Windrush Press.

-Young, Peter; Holmes, Richard (2000) [First published 1974], The English Civil War, Ware: Wordsworth Editions.

-Winder, Robert (9 May 1999), "It's a grand life for Chelsea's men in scarlet", The Independent.

-Scott, C.L.; Turton, A; Gruber von Arni, E. (2004), Edgehill: The Battle Reinterpreted, Barnsley, South Yorkshire: Pen & Sword Military.

-Tony Pollard, Neil Oliver (2003), "Edgehill", Two Men in a Trench II, London: Michael Joseph.

-Foard, Glenn (2012), "The Battle of Edgehill 1642: a case study", Battlefield Archaeology of the English Civil War, BAR British Series 570, Oxford: Archaeopress.

-William Seymour: Battles in Britain and their political background. 1066-1746. Wordsworth Editions, Ware 1997.

-Christopher L. Scott, Alan Turton, Eric Gruber von Arni: Edgehill. The Battle Reinterpreted. Pen & Sword Military, Barnsley 2004.

-The UK Battlefieds Resource Center: The Battlefields Trust, Meadow Cottage, 33 High Green, Brooke, Norwich, NR15 1HR

Gavin Bott, Executive Producer: Line of Fire: Battle of Edgehill. (2006) History International Channel U.S.

-Ashley, Maurice. The English Civil War. Sutton. (1990)

-Bennett, Martyn. Historical Dictionary of the British and Irish Civil Wars 1637–1660 (Scarecrow Press, 1999).

-Clarendon. History of the Rebellion and Civil Wars in England: Begun in the Year 1641 by Edward Hyde, 1st Earl of Clarendon (1717): Volume I, Part 1, Volume I, Part 2, Volume II, Part 1, Volume II, Part 2, Volume III, Part 1, Volume III, Part 2

-The Life of Edward, Earl of Clarendon, in which is included a Continuation of his History of the Grand Rebellion by Edward Hyde, 1st Earl of Clarendon (Clarendon Press, 1827): Volume I, Volume II, Volume III

-Cust, Richard, and Ann Hughes, eds. The English Civil War (Arnold, 1997), emphasis on historiography.

-Gardiner, Samuel Rawson. History of the Great Civil War, 1642–1649 (1886–1901): Volume I (1642–1644); Volume II (1644–1647); Volume III (1645–1647); Volume IV (1647–1649), The basic narrative history used by all other scholars.

-Gaunt, Peter. The English Civil War: A Military History (2014) online review

-Ludlow, Edmund (1894), C.H. Firth, ed., The Memoirs of Edmund Ludlow Lieutenant-General of the Horse in the Army of the Commonwealth of England 1625–1672, Oxford: Clarendon Press

-Morrill, John. The nature of the English Revolution (Routledge, 2014), 20 essays by Morrill.

-Prior, Charles W.A. and Glenn Burgess, eds. England's wars of religion, revisited (Ashgate, 2013). 14 scholars discuss the argument of John Morrill that the English Civil War was the last war of religion, rather than the first modern revolution. excerpt; historiography pp. 1–25.

-Scott, Jonathan (2000), England's Troubles: Seventeenth-century English political instability in European context, Cambridge University Press, – "Jonathan Scott's major reinterpretation of the seventeenth century ... England's crisis is viewed in European perspective" (Morgan, Hiram (March 2001), "review", journal of Historical Research, doi:10.14296/RiH/issn.1749.8155).

-Wiemann, Dirk, ed. Perspectives on English Revolutionary Republicanism (Routledge, 2016).

-Woolrych, Austin. Britain in revolution: 1625–1660 (Oxford UP, 2002).

WIT

HIS

www.ingramcontent.com/pod-product-compliance
Ingram Content Group UK Ltd.
Pitfield, Milton Keynes, MK11 3LW, UK
UKHW050147280726
14058UKWH00007B/871